Abraham's Ashes

The Absurdity of Monotheism

Peter Heinegg

University Press of America,® Inc.
Lanham • Boulder • New York • Toronto • Plymouth, UK

Copyright © 2013 by University Press of America,® Inc.
4501 Forbes Boulevard, Suite 200, Lanham, Maryland 20706
UPA Aquisitions Department (301) 459-3366

10 Thornbury Road, Plymouth PL6 7PP, United Kingdom

All rights reserved

British Library Cataloguing in Publication Information Available

Library of Congress Control Number: 2012941673
ISBN: 978-0-7618-5965-9

Approximately 795 words from THE KORAN translated by N. J. Dawood (Penguin Classics 1956, Fifth revised edition 1990). Copyright © N. J. Dawood, 1956, 1959, 1966, 1968, 1974, 1990, 1993, 1997, 1999, 2003, 2006.

In memory of my grandfather,
Franz Fabry (Feilchenfeld)
1888-1967

Contents

Prelude	vii
Acknowledgments	xi
Introduction: Crazy Abe	1
1 A Bad Beginning	25
2 The Son Who *Was* Sacrificed	47
3 Abraham, the First Muslim	67
Conclusion: Farewell to the Lunacy	87

Prelude

Blessed Are the Abrahamic Bootlickers (Not)

    Fly round the world, from pole to pole,
    and watch this awe-full scene unfold:
    face down, hands out, butts in the air,
    the pious masses bend in prayer—
    or humbly fawn with lowered tail
    like wolves before the alpha male,
    or bow their heads or bend their knees,
    or beat their breasts, to urge their pleas
    to Yahweh, Allah, Jesus, Lord,
    the Grand, the Good, the All-Adored.

    One long religious roundelay:
    O parce nobis, Domine *   (*Lat. Spare us, o Lord)
    or *Kyrie, eleison,* †   (†Grk. Lord, have mercy)
    khoneyni ‡ adds some Jewish tone.   (‡Heb. Have mercy on me)
    Of course, it's wholly infantile,
    but, non-believers, don't just smile.
    We have to find some logic here,
    some *cui bono*, love or fear,
    to crack this huge latreutic case—
    why worshipers stare into space
    prostrate themselves, crouch, kowtow, grovel.

Why heap up slavish praise, then shovel
it into God's voracious maw?
The pious say, "Why? It's the Law!"
But that won't do—try these four schemes
(We'll call them Adoration's Memes):

First, God's an Egomaniac,
a Junkie—worship is his crack.
So bring it on! And, man, they do:
salaams, hosannahs, hallelujahs, hymns, the holy-rolling stuff;
all His enablers pour out puff-
ery non-stop to feed his habit.
He just can't get enough—dagnabit!

Or, Second, maybe God's sadistic
(that sounds a bit more realistic):
He loves to watch his creatures squirm
(not man the titan, man the worm).
Folks twist and writhe amid the dust:
it's vaguely similar to lust:
a desperate, pathetic passion,
a belly-flop without the splashin').
And, best of all, he doesn't listen!
All those requests somehow go missin'.
Hope springs eternal, Pope would say;
and if Godot can't come today,
perhaps we'll see his face *demain*.
You never know: *peut-être, hein*?

Sure, sure, you keep on hoping, friend:
he's just beyond the rainbow's end,
the big rock-candy mount (and, oh,
that fountain now spouts Veuve Clicquot).
But wait, this line is far too sick.
Screw *Schadenfreude*—why not pick

the Third Proposal: don't assault

His Majesty, it's *humans*' fault.
While pray-ers prate their yadda-yadda,
the truth is, way up there lies … nada.
God's not to blame, that isn't fair;
mirages, phantoms, mere hot air
bear no responsibility
for what deluded viewers "see."
So this is self-delusion? Yup,
a bunch of loonies thought it up;
and other loonies form the chorus
(we try to reason—they ignore us).
Well, leave them in their stagnant pool
of tears and fears and godly foolishness: they seem to like it. Oy,
it sounds like masochistic joy.

Wait, that would be our Number Four:
believers need to pay much more
than life's already hefty price.
Their sufferings add extra spice.
Let's see: their guilt, their wasted time,
their feeling that they're sinful slime,
their silent God, their vain petitions
for help and love, their strong suspicions
that He's not there, their holy terrors
(eternal hell for moral errors),
and on and on. Egad, why bother
with all this ditzy "Lord! Lord!" pother.
Must be, believers *dig* their pains—
the deadly God-drug's fried their brains

All true, and yet believers claim,
"We do feel *something*, all the same.
There's *something* going on inside
our hearts and souls; it's like a tide
(a wind?) of in-spir-ation!"
No, actually it's masturbation.
It's self-provoked neuronal jollies,

a praying-hands-job, theo-follies.
(Bernini's St. Teresa's wound,
so sweetly painful that she swooned).

Oh well, no need to start a fight—
whatever gets you through the night,
I guess. But really, why not keep
your wits—and tell that "Lord" to bleep
himself and all the fraud that taints
the playpen antics of the saints?
There has to be a better way;
you bet, and it's called *sapere*
("wise up" in Latin), use your head,
don't die upstairs before you're dead,
don't talk to spooks, don't wail and whine
to *anything* purportedly divine.
Your mind was meant for better things
than non-existent sky-throned kings.
Don't lose your self-respect—just look:
bootlickers' mouths are filled with gook.

—Peter Heinegg

Acknowledgments

Thanks to Penguin Books for permission to quote from *The Koran*, tr. N. J. Dawood. All Bible quotations, unless otherwise indicated, are from the King James Version. All other translations, unless otherwise indicated, are by the author.

Introduction

Crazy Abe

When a man's fancy gets astride on his reason, when imagination is at cuffs with the senses, and common understanding, as well as common sense, is kicked out of doors, the first proselyte he makes is himself; and when that is once compassed, the difficulty is not so great in bringing over others; a strong delusion always operating from without as vigorously as from within. For cant and vision are to the ear and the eye, the same that tickling is to the touch. Those entertainments and pleasures we most value in life, are such as dupe and play the wag with the senses. For, if we take an examination of what is generally understood by happiness, as it has respect either to the understanding or the senses, we shall find all its properties and adjuncts will herd under this short definition, that it is a perpetual possession of being well deceived.

—Jonathan Swift, *A Tale of a Tub*, "A Digression on Madness" (1704)

We know approximately when and by what kinds of men religious doctrines were created. If in addition we discover the motives which led to this, our attitude to the problems of religion will undergo a marked displacement. We shall tell ourselves that it would be very nice if there were a God who created the world, and if there was a benevolent Providence, and if there was a moral order in the universe and an after-life; but it is a very striking fact that all this is exactly as we are bound to wish it to be. And it would be more remarkable still if our wretched, ignorant and downtrodden ancestors had succeeded in solving all these difficult riddles of the universe.

—Sigmund Freud, *The Future of an Illusion* (1927), tr. James Strachey

Reading Holy Writ is always a risky business. You expect, at least initially, to be edified; and instead you're all too often appalled. Even if not a believer, you anticipate being impressed, at least by the "Bible-as-literature," and instead you get depressed. You expect to see "transcendence"; but you find yourself stuck in the same old all-too-human mud puddle. Take the story of Abraham, whom Jews, Christians, and Muslims have been pleased to call the Father of their faith. For countless centuries monotheists have been meditating on, and proclaiming, his greatness—but apparently without paying much attention to his "biography." So, before criticizing the tenets, practices, and mind-set of the One-Godders, we need to look at their hero.

We first meet Abram (the future Abraham) in Genesis 11, when he moves with the rest of his family from "Ur of the Chaldeans" (in modern-day Iraq) to Haran, near today's Turkish-Syrian border . Then in Chapter 12.1-4, after his father Terah dies, Abram gets the mysterious, world-famous call: "Now the LORD had said unto Abram, Get thee out of thy country, and from thy kindred, and from thy father's house, unto a land that I will show thee: And I will make of thee a great nation, and I will bless thee, and make thy name great; and thou shalt be a blessing. And I will bless them that bless thee and curse him that curseth thee; and in thee shall all families of the earth be blessed. So Abram departed, as the LORD had spoken unto him."

What's going on here? At the moment that might well qualify as the birth of monotheism (or monolatry or henotheism), we run into something close to an absolute blank. Who is "the LORD"? The word itself, the conventional English translation for YHWH, isn't (partially) explained until Moses sees the burning bush on Mt. Sinai/Horeb, where God identifies himself as (something like) "I Am Who Am," "I Am," or "I Am the One Who Brings Into Being." Scholars are still wrestling with that one. In any case, the name itself tells us almost nothing about the Speaker, who reveals his nature, insofar as "he" has one, not philosophically through definitions but existentially through muscular interventions in human affairs. More on that later.

The LORD tells Abram to get out (the endlessly celebrated *lekh lekha* [literally "leave for you"]). Why his plans for Abram and his descendants require his departure from Haran isn't made clear; though later tradition portrayed the place as polluted with idolatry. In Joshua 24.2 Moses' moribund successor reminds the Israelites that their "fathers" (Terah's whole family) "served other gods." In the Qur'an 6:74 Abraham asks his father (named Azar, not Terah), "Will you worship idols as your gods? Surely you and all your people are in palpable error." That would be a logical motive for Abram's departure; but Genesis doesn't mention it. In any case, the spectacular but unearned promises that follow come literally out of nowhere.

For no reason at all God tells Abram that He'll be giving this nomadic sheikh a new homeland and all sorts of attendant greatness. This bonanza will *not* be a reward for personal virtue (which is in short supply among the patriarchs of Israel) or any sort of extraordinary human achievement, but just because. Of course, it might be objected that God failed to fulfill all of his promise, since, however much fame Abraham later won and however much the monotheistic tradition could be viewed as a grand international blessing, Israel itself never qualified as a "great nation." Although its survival as a polity after millennia of conquest and persecution might be seen as a miracle, it has always been quite small, weak, and, *Realpolitik*-ally speaking, insignificant.

But what is one to make of this world-historical windfall? Claims of being the "chosen people" have long rankled with critics of Israel (and anti-Semites), even though, as we'll see, the Bible also stresses a number of humility-inducing counter-themes. But while many Christians and Muslims have attacked this supposed Jewish pride and exclusivity, their own religions have borrowed and internalized the same notion of being God's special favorites—while they angrily accuse the Hebrews/Israelites/Jews of having forfeited their privileged position by being "stiff-necked and uncircumcised of heart and ears" (Acts 7.51) or some such vice.

In any event, God, whoever he is, has chosen Abram and guaranteed him and his offspring a glorious future. Obedient to Yahweh's command, he moves from Haran into Canaan, where he's specifically informed that his "seed" will—again, for no special reason—eventually be given the land inhabited by the Canaanites. (By the way, it might be noticed that this familiar metaphor for "offspring" has the disadvantage of reducing the female genetic component to a kind of potting soil or petri dish, a minor symptom of the massive sexism that will blight all three Abrahamic religions.)

Forced by a famine to move down into Egypt, Abram saves his own skin by pretending that his beautiful wife Sarai is his sister (she is in fact his half-sister). This leads to the first of his two spousal giveaways, which lands Sarai in Pharaoh's harem—until God sends "great plagues" down on Pharaoh and his house; and the chastened monarch returns Sarai to her husband. This sort of unheroic behavior, which Voltaire enjoyed mocking in his *Dictionnaire*

Philosophique (1764), may actually strike contemporary readers as refreshing, insofar as it suggests the biblical sources are making no attempt to idealize or prettify revered figures from the past, as hagiography generally does.

In Chapter 13 Abram's relationship with The LORD grows more intense through a succession of theophanies (there will be seven of these obscurely described encounters) and building altars to his new deity. Abram "settles" in Canaan, although as a pastoralist he'll have to keep moving with his flocks and herds. Genesis characterizes Abram as a rich chieftain, powerful enough to lead a raiding party of 318 men to rescue his nephew Lot from a group of local "kings," headed by Chedorlaomer of Elam. One wonders if Muhammad, himself a military man and occasional brigand, ever heard of this adventure. In any case, there would be many more holy warriors (mostly fantasized) in the Old Testament; and countless real-life Christian and Muslim captains giving violent expression to their faith once, like Abraham, they could muster enough soldiers to do some damage.

In Chapter 15 the LORD maintains his pattern of encouraging visitations to Abram, who now raises for the first time the problem of his childlessness. Not to worry, God insists, and with perhaps pardonable exaggeration tells him, "Look now toward heaven, and tell [count] the stars, if thou be able to number them; and he said unto him, so shall thy seed be" (v. 5). Abram believes, i.e., trusts his divine partner; and the Lord "counted it to him for righteousness" (v. 6). That phrase would, we know, have a fabulous future as a religious mantra—despite its ambiguousness (did "counted for" mean "a reasonable facsimile"? "a condescendingly accepted substitute"? "the best that could be hoped for from a wretched human"?) St. Paul would build a whole theology on it; and Muhammad would divide the world into believers and non-believers, with a heavenly or hellish life after death awaiting them: Be like Abraham—or else.

To seal this recurrent deal, Abram sacrifices a heifer, a nanny goat, a ram, a turtledove and a young pigeon, thereby inaugurating the sacred rite of monotheistic animal butchery, which was carried out in the Temple of Jerusalem until 70 CE and may yet get reinstated if and when the Temple is. Christians, in their desire to break away from all-too-onerous ceremonies of Judaism, got rid of such sacrifices, but flung wide the gates of carnivorousness by declaring all meat and seafood kosher, while Muslims happily continue the custom in the uproarious bloodbath of Eid al-Adha (see Chapter Three).

In Chapter 16 the desperate, childless Sarai offers her slave girl to Abram, evidently hoping that any child born to the Egyptian woman would somehow qualify as hers. Here it's worth noticing that just as male "seed" in the Bible (and the Qur'an) does all the heavy lifting of generation, there is no such thing as male infertility, as the later stories of Rebekah, Rachel, the (nameless) mother of Samson, and Hannah will show. And, needless to say, when the LORD relieves their sterility, the resulting baby is always a boy, as with the gynecologically-impossible conceptions of Elizabeth and Mary in the New Testament.

Predictably enough, once Hagar becomes pregnant, she starts acting uppity toward Sarai, which prompts her antagonized mistress to drive her off. The spineless Abram has no objection ("do to her as it pleaseth thee," 16.6); but the runaway slave-girl is rescued by an angel of the LORD, who tells her to head back and predicts that she'll give birth to a son and be the ancestress of a vast multitude. And so Ishmael (Ismail for Muslims) is born, although when Sarai eventually gives birth to Isaac, she'll again pressure Abram/Abraham to expel her hated competitor (21.9-21). Cruel as the action seems, God approves of it, and tells Abraham, "In all that Sarah hath said unto thee, hearken to her voice; for in Isaac shall thy seed be called" (v. 12). This time Hagar and son are dispatched for good; but the always helpful angel of God saves them from dying of thirst in the wilderness, and again promises a fine future for her progeny, if nothing like the splendors awaiting the line of Isaac.

Abraham is now down to one wife, and a very old one at that; but at some point after this he marries Keturah (25.1), by whom he has six sons, the ancestors of the Arabian tribes. Any daughters he may have had go unmentioned, even as his concubines (25.1) and their sons are neither named nor numbered, since they're by definition irrelevant. But if nothing else, Abraham's familial adventures laid the foundation of patriarchal polygyny, which flourishes to this day. In the year 1000 CE rabbi Gershom ben Judah officially banned plural wives for Ashkenazi Jews, though some Sephardis, especially in Muslim countries, may continue the practice. Muhammad, of course, welcomed the tradition, as have countless rich Muslims after him. With its unmarried Messiah and its cult of celibacy, Christianity had no truck with polygamy; and any Christian harems, with brief exceptions such as the first Mormons and their current fundamentalist brethren, had to be operated in secret. But all the Abrahamic religions could, and did, agree that women were essentially breeders; and apart from that role, as we'll see, they were condemned to the role of household helpers, as the famous poem honoring the "good wife" or "virtuous woman" in Proverbs 31 makes clear.

In the pivotal Chapter 17 of Genesis, the LORD announces that Abram (possibly meaning "exalted father") has had his name changed to Abraham (perhaps "father of a multitude"). Sarai will become Sarah, although both names seem to mean the same thing, "princess"; and Yahweh doesn't bother to tell Sarah this himself, but has Abraham pass the word on. A divinely initiated change of one's name brings a change of one's identity, as in the shift from Jacob to Israel; and it's part of monotheism's central meme: prophecy. Starting with Abraham, and modeling themselves on his example, all sorts of inspired people, i.e., men, will claim that in some unfathomable fashion the LORD, the Most High, the Eternal One, whatever you want to call him, has spoken to them; and that hence their reports of those conversations are unquestionably true and incredibly important. It doesn't matter whether the contents of that divine-human tête-à-tête make empirical sense or not; it doesn't matter whether such rapturous interchanges are even vaguely historical; and it doesn't matter whether the human prophet actually existed—numerous biblical scholars have questioned the existence of Abraham, among other scriptural heroes. But even if he never lived, Abraham had a glorious post-mortem career, which deserves our attention.

Actually, a prophet whose existence is beyond dispute can be much messier than a (perhaps) fictional one: consider all the headaches endured by the followers of such dubious characters as Sabbatai Zevi, Joseph Smith, Elijah Mohammed, et al. What counts is that some person or group, has caught a whiff of ozone-charged theophanic air and can't stop talking about it. Psychic disturbance equals revelation equals eternal truth—and, all too frequently, death to those who disagree. The fear-laden ferocity of calls to faith is directly proportional to their factual baselessness. We'll see a lot of that in our travels through the Abrahamic landscape.

God now wants to formalize his relations with Abraham's clan by means of a covenant, which in turn will be sealed by circumcision. The most obvious thing about this timeless ritual, which the ancient Hebrews borrowed from earlier Canaanite cultures and then projected back to the time of their ancestors, is that it excludes women. Women make the babies, but men carry on the covenant; and anyone without a circumcised penis is at best a second-class citizen. Hence the Temple's priests and the synagogue's rabbis and the mosques' mullahs will have to be men, like the entire Catholic clergy. The Fathers wouldn't have it any other way. What kind of farmer would you be (and agriculture is the first and archetypal technology) without a large supply of seed?

What the ceremony means beyond that has been subject to nonstop speculation. Maimonides thought it reduced sexual desire, which adds a soupçon of ironic amusement to the fact that nowadays practically all goyishe male porn stars are circumcised. A feeble rationalization one sometimes hears from modern Jews is that it was a hygienic measure (even as the ban on pork prevented trichinosis), resulting in less cervical cancer and, best of all, slowing the transmission of AIDS. But that's wishful, anachronistic thinking. Clearly, the point was to create a powerful bond between the individual male and the religious community, in a sort of variant on the pre-redeemed Charles Colson's axiom that, "When you've got them by the balls, their hearts and minds will follow." The genitals are in the literal center of the body; and every time a man or boy looks at or touches his private parts, he's reminded of his belonging-through-severance. Whether circumcision implies the threat of castration may be doubted, though it's hardly impossible.

At this point God tells Abraham that his son will be named Isaac, "he laughs," an allusion to incredulous reactions of both the 99-year-old Abraham and the 90-year-old and long-since-postmenopausal Sarah to the news of the coming pregnancy. Actually, at first nobody bothers to inform Sarah about it. Like a proper Bedouin wife, she's hidden away in her tent and simply eavesdrops on the discussion between Abraham and the celestial messenger. The same kind of thing happens in Matthew's account of the "Incarnation" (1.18-25), where Joseph, but not Mary, receives advance word of the miraculous birth about to take place.

Abraham learns of his impossible fatherhood during the theophany at the oaks of Mamre (Gen. 18), where "three men," who sound more like angels, morph into the LORD himself. Abraham is further told about the proximate nuking of Sodom and Gomorrah for their "very grievous sin." He then famously bargains with God, and comes away with the promise that the cities will be spared if as many as ten just men (as always, not people, "men," a Canaanite minyan) can be found. Unfortunately, they can't, as we see in the episode of the attempted rape of the angels by the Sodomites, and so the cities are completely destroyed by fire from heaven. Since the sin in question is presumably gay sex, one can't help feeling perplexed by the way that the countless children and inoffensive heterosexuals in town had to be annihilated along with the hardened sinners. But one of the features of monotheism is its penchant for assigning corporate guilt.

Just as God's favorites get lumped together (cf. Isaiah 60.21, "Thy people shall all be righteous: they shall inherit the land forever, the branch of my planting, the work of my hands, that I may be glorified"), so do the "wicked." The prophets adore categorical statements and summary judgments—no wimpy phrases like "on the whole," "a considerable minority, or "a high percentage of you." "From the least of them even unto the greatest of them," says Jeremiah in 6.17, "every one is given to covetousness, and from the prophet even unto the priest every one dealeth falsely." So "Sodom" has sinned, collectively and totally; and down it goes.

In monotheistic morality you can't get much wickeder than "Sodomites." The Torah (Lev. 20.13) prescribes the death penalty for male homosexual acts, although it's not certain that this was ever carried out. Practically all Christian countries criminalized homosexuality until a generation or two ago. The Qur'an vituperates the "people of Lot," and in the hadiths Muhammad positively curses them. Given Abrahamic patriarchalism and God-drunk natalism, it figures: Many, if not most, gays show a limited interested in impregnating women. By the same token, the various sacred texts (though not St. Paul) mostly ignore lesbianism; since women had no control over their bodies and would be forced to breed, like it or not. Even as liberal Judaism and Christianity are now moving toward full acceptance of gays, however flatly that contradicts their oldest traditions, conservative believers are still fulminating against, and in some Sharia-ridden lands, stoning homosexuals (the Christian Taliban usually stop short of murder). It's God's will. "Then the LORD rained upon Sodom and upon Gomorrah brimstone and fire from the LORD out of heaven. And he overthrew those cities, and all the plain, and all the inhabitants of the cities, and that which grew upon the ground" (19.24-25).

The story ends with a characteristic ethnic slur, when Lot's (unnamed) daughters, mistakenly believing that no other men had survived the cataclysm, get their father drunk and copulate with him, later giving birth to two (male, of course) incestuous bastards, Moab and Ben-Ammi, who turn out to be the eponymous ancestors of two of Israel's worst future enemies, the Moabites and Ammonites. So there! Once more we have the evil others, the goyim, the pagans, the kaffirs, the unclean, the unbaptized, the unconverted. Present-day ecumenists are trying to wriggle out of this contemptuous us-them dichotomy by stressing the (often marginal) counter-traditions of inclusiveness and tolerance. One can only hope they succeed, but it's going against the grain. Monotheistic faiths don't want to be seen as mere competing, much less roughly equal, products in the ideological marketplace.

Meanwhile, in Chapter 20 we seem to be flying back in time (or else simply to a different, "Elohistic" source), since Abraham, gives his wife away again, to King Abimelech of Gerar, which presumes that she's still a hot commodity. But God saves the day again, by telling Abimelech, a decent fellow, the truth about Sarah—and striking his harem with sterility. In Chapter 21, as mentioned, Sarah once again turns on Hagar, and drives her and her son Ishmael off into the wilderness—for good. As so often, the Hebrew Bible doesn't mind portraying its protagonists in a downright ugly light.

In Chapter 22, the so-called "Binding of Isaac," we witness the absolute worst moment of Abraham's life and one of most repellent scenes in the Bible. (See Erich Auerbach's *Mimesis* for a classic—

and non-judgmental—literary analysis of the text.) Out of nowhere God commands Abraham, "Take now thine only son, Isaac, whom thou lovest [a nice touch: I know just how much this is going to pain you], and get thee into the land of Moriah, and offer him there for a burnt offering upon one of the mountains which I shall tell you of' (v. 2). What in heaven's name is going on here?

The age-old explanation, and the one apparently intended by the unknown storyteller(s), that this is a strenuous test of faith, which culminates with a divine "Just kidding!," won't wash, for a number of reasons. Astonishingly, Abraham, who was so eager to dicker with God over the fate of Sodom, says nothing here and meekly heads out on his three-day journey. This suggests, among other things, that if the story has any basis in history, child-sacrifice was a familiar feature of life at the time. The Bible frequently complains about the cult of Molech (though its exact nature remains the subject of fierce controversy); and two kings of Judah, Ahaz (ca. 735-715 BCE) and Manasseh (ca. 687-642 BCE) are accused of "passing their sons through the fire."

Abraham, of course, gets off the hook when the angel of the LORD tells him to desist and supplies him with a ram as a substitute offering. That lucky turnabout carries us forward to the Exodus, where God butchers all the firstborn sons (and bull calves!) of Egypt, while the Israelites are spared, because in another divinely engineered substitution, they smear the lintels and doorposts of their dwellings with the blood of the (male) Paschal lamb. The bottom line here is that God owns all life and wants his share of it. In Exodus 13. 2, he tells Moses, "Sanctify unto me all the firstborn, whatsoever openeth the womb among the children of Israel, both of man and of beast: it is mine."

What this comes down to is, "Every firstling of an ass thou shalt redeem with a lamb; and if you wilt not redeem it, then thou shalt break his neck: and all the firstborn of man among thy children shalt thou redeem (v. 13).This idea is kept alive today in the Jewish ceremony of *pidyon ha-ben,* the "redemption" of the firstborn son: On the thirty-first day after the birth of a boy, the child is "bought back" from God by a symbolic payment of five silver shekels (see "Firstborn, Redemption of the," in *The Oxford Dictionary of the Jewish Religion,* 1997). Putting it another way, the life of all the firstborn male (i.e., most prized) offspring is forfeit to God and has to be negotiated for.

This gruesome thought will enjoy a long career in Christianity, where Jesus' death on the cross somehow "redeems" the sinful masses of mere humanity. We'll examine the confused theology of "Redemption" more explicitly in Chapter Two; but the general scheme of substitution of one life for another, or many others, seems transparent—if still hideous—enough. After all, once Abraham had passed the LORD's sadistic test, why couldn't God have simply said, "Good job! Have a nice day!"? Why drag in the poor ram? (All monotheistic religions are big fans of animal cruelty, as we'll see.) The gods, the Aztecs were quoted as saying, are thirsty for blood; and this one surely is.

Jews, Christians, and Muslims in various ways have enthusiastically embraced the near-murder of Isaac. The story of the Aqedah forms part of the morning prayer, or shaharit, recited every day in the synagogue. Christians always associated Isaac with Jesus, who goes the Old Testament one better by sacrificing *himself* in response to God's inscrutable command. Kierkegaard sought to dampen the shock to modern sensibilities with his presto-change-o notion, "the teleological suspension of the ethical," which boils down to the old "God's the boss, he can do what he wants," although many people would argue that anyone who "suspends the ethical" must himself be unethical.

Muslims too love the tale, although most of them insist it was Ishmael, not Isaac, who was so close to death. In Muhammad's retelling, however, it loses most of its power; since narrative never was the Prophet's forte: After Abraham/Ibrahim asks Allah for a "righteous son," he gets one, Ishmael/Ismail. "We [God] gave him news of a gentle [or patient] son. And when he reached the age when he could work with him, his father said to him, 'My son. I dreamt that I was sacrificing you. Tell me what you think.' He replied: 'Father, do as you are bidden. God willing, you shall find me steadfast.' And when they had both submitted to God, and Abraham had laid down his son prostrate on his face, We called out to him, saying: 'Abraham, you have fulfilled your vision.' Thus do we reward the righteous. That was indeed a bitter test. We ransomed his son with a noble sacrifice and bestowed on him the praise of later generations" (37:101-108).

Muslims celebrate the event in the feast of Eidh al-Adh, where gigantic hecatombs of cows, sheep, and goats are slaughtered in happy recollection of the original victim-substitution (Chapter Three). Islamic tradition has added a number of details to Abraham's story in general, and the binding of Isaac in particular. Among these are Satan's tempting of the distressed father to back out of his promise to God, which Abraham fights off by flinging stones at the Devil—an action imitated by pilgrims on the hajj to this day and enormously effective, according to the believers who have tried it. The figure of the Accuser plays a very small role in the Old Testament; but he got a major career boost (or was it mission-creep?) in the N.T. and the Qur'an, as will be seen later on.

At this point a brief psycho-theological excursus might be in order; the Binding of Isaac seems to have a lot of Oedipal, or rather Laian-Oedipal, overtones (since it was Laius who wanted his son dead and deliberately tried to kill him, and the accidental parricide Oedipus who wished and thereby brought death upon *his* sons Eteocles and Polynices). God in Genesis has a deep filicidal streak. He condemns all of humanity to eventual death after the first couple's disobedience. He murders practically all his children in the Flood; and he nukes every last person in Sodom and Gomorrah. He flirts with the idea of a double-filicide in the Binding of Isaac, since having the old man kill his son (the child who "counts") would in a real way kill both of them. In any case, he needs to show that he has the right and the power to annihilate his (male) children—something his chosen people will never forget because of the *pidyon haben*. That should show everybody who's in charge. Of course, since the Heavenly Father doesn't exist, it would be more accurate to say that human males are just projecting their own domination and rage onto their God, who thereby sanctifies it.

Things get even stickier with Jesus and *his* Father. In sending the Messiah to his death, God might look little better than an executioner, though in Book III of *Paradise Lost* Milton prefers making Jesus a heroic volunteer for the greatest of good causes. Then again, the Father might have volunteered himself, but that would called for completely rewriting the New Testament. So Jesus dies (lovingly) because his Father (lovingly) wants him to. All covenants need blood, and this one does too. Then Christians symbolically unite themselves with the Supreme Victim, and like him die and rise from the dead, right now (in spirit) and later too, at the end of time (in the flesh).

What are we to make of Calvary? That the Father was jealous of the way his Son would displace him from the center of attention, and thus wanted him to at least pay a high price for his usurpation? (The crucifixion as an initiation rite?) On a more jejune level, countless preachers and teachers have presented Jesus as a divine-human shield taking a bullet for the rest of us, who deserved to die for our sins and whom God the Father, simply as a matter of justice, wanted (was bound) to punish. By God, somebody's got to placate The Old Man. The key to being a Christian is to accept that substitutionary atonement and thrive on it. Are you washed in the blood of the Lamb? I mean, the pool's already there; just dive in. If not, you're out of luck.

Muhammad, of course, indignantly rejected all that Redemption-talk. Jesus was just a regular prophet. In 39:62 he says that the faithful "have earned salvation," a line that orthodox Christians would blanch at. But Allah is very much a killer, and he continues to tout his homicidal record throughout the Qur'an. In a typical passage, he notes, "The tribes of 'Ad and Thamud were also destroyed, and so were those who dwelt at Rass, and many generations in between. To each of them We gave examples, and each of them We exterminated" (25:39). And the sadistic prophet echoes his Lord: "Thamud and 'Ad denied the Last Judgment. By a deafening shout was Thamud destroyed, and 'Ad by a howling, violent gale which He let loose on them for seven nights and eight successive days: you might have seen them lying dead as though they had been hollow trunks of palm trees. Can you see even one of them alive?" (69:2-8). As in the Old and New Testaments, God's infinite compassion sometimes gets switched off. The mere sight of a place like Sodom could make him see red.

No surprise here, since as usual the prophet and his God are one and the same. Notice how Allah's satisfaction in condemning a sinner to the tortures of Hell segues immediately into divine praise of Muhammad: "We shall say: 'Lay hold of him [the doomed sinner] and bind him. Burn him in the fire of Hell, then fasten him with a chain seventy cubits long. For he did not believe in God, the Most Great, nor did he care to feed the desolate. Today he shall be friendless here; only filth shall be his food, the filth which only sinners eat.' ... this is the utterance of a noble messenger. It is no poet's speech: scant is your faith! It is no soothsayer's divination: how little you reflect! It is a revelation of the Lord of the Universe" (69:40-43). It's the prophet-as-ventriloquist, with his invisible puppet-god.

There's nothing uniquely egotistical about all this. The vast majority of humans never experience God except in some pallid, borrowed or imitative fashion (though the sense of togetherness with other worshipers can be powerful). They have to lean on the testimony, real or imagined, of the prophets, who are too crazy themselves to tell the difference between the two. They feel the hot blasts of their own rage, contempt, and fury pouring out of God's nostrils. So why shouldn't they enjoy the highs, whether fueled by happiness or hatred, that they're sometimes "granted," which in a feedback loop afford them still more nervous excitement, ecstatic exaltation, enhanced self-worth, and public attention (even persecution, up to a point, can be flattering).

They're the *only* spokesmen of an otherwise silent God. Without them, how would we know about creation, redemption, God's will for us, heaven, hell, all that good stuff? Of course, if an actual person told us the story of the Aqedah, we'd immediately write it off as fiction. But when religion comes up, the almost universal convention is to nod politely and drop all standards of verisimilitude. It's the least we can do for our brothers and sisters in the various "communities of faith" around the world. In Academe and journalism, convention demands that outsiders report with unquestioning poker faces the palpable nonsense uttered by monotheists. Do Jews believe the Messiah will come (perhaps any day now)? Do Catholics believe in transubstantiation? Do Muslims believe the angel Jibril dictated the Qur'an to Muhammad? Do Mormons believe that there really *were* golden plates inscribed in "Reformed Egyptian"? Absolutely, why not, no problem—after all, if God could let Abraham stew for three days in the horrific anticipation of murdering Isaac ...

Which takes us back to Yahweh's "April fool!" moment with Abraham": once Isaac is spared, Abraham's job, as far as Genesis goes, is more or less done. He does, though, have to find a non-Canaanite wife for Isaac, a mission successfully carried out by his eldest, but unnamed servant. The finding and wooing of Rebekah, the daughter of Abraham's cousin Bethuel, makes a pleasant idyllic interlude, though some modern readers are likely to be distracted by the curious oath that Abraham, makes his servant take before leaving for Mesopotamia: the man is told to place his hand under

Abraham's genitals as he swears to conduct the bride-search in Abraham's original land.

It stands to reason: There's nothing more sacred and solemn in the male body than testicles. Eunuchs were banned [Deut. 23.2] from the worshiping community of Israel; and on the whole they've gotten a bad reception in the monotheistic world. Jesus clearly meant to shock his audience when he put in a good word for those who make themselves eunuchs for the kingdom of heaven (Mt. 19.12); but, other than Origen, the Russian Skoptsi, and some other fanatics, literal self-castration has gone nowhere in Christianity. And Catholic vows of clerical celibacy, even when kept, have proved to be no bar to all the usual kinds of male chauvinistic piggery. Abraham may not have been a macho man, in the standard sense—e.g., his cowardly abandonment of Sarah or his inability to resist Sarah's cruelty to Hagar—but with his phenomenally fertile (in the long run) "seed," he gave monotheistic machismo a fine start.

In Chapter 25, after the mention of Keturah and her brood, Abraham has a quiet death. "And these are the days of the years of Abraham's life which he lived, an hundred threescore and fifteen years. Then Abraham gave up the ghost, and died in a good old age, an old man, and full of years, and was gathered to his people" (vv.7-8). So he died, and stayed dead; but later Judaism, and, *a fortiori*, Christianity and Islam, wouldn't settle for that. Though the great bulk of the Hebrew Bible has no faith, and little interest, in life beyond the grave (Psalm 115.17 notes laconically that, "The dead praise not the LORD, neither any that go down into silence"), contact with Persian and Platonic conceptions of the afterlife, along with repeated bitter experience that the Deuteronomic principle (do well/fare well, here and now) was inoperative, led Jews to change their tune. Thus they began to imagine the World To Come as a place of final judgment, rewards and punishments.

Despite this, Jews as a group, unlike their Christian and Muslim brothers, never developed much passion for the *olam ha-ba*—and they still tend to ignore it. But Jesus, and even more Muhammad, and their followers couldn't get enough of the afterlife, whence the stream of baseless Technicolor fantasies about our post-mortem doings. "Abraham's bosom" later became a synonym for heaven (Luke 16.22,-23), but the story of Abraham in Genesis has no need of a heavenly epilogue. God proved to be Abraham's reliable friend and supporter through his very long life (an obvious symbol and form of earthly fulfillment); he could bank on the LORD'S promises, and by purchasing Sarah's grave (Gen. 23) in the field and cave of Machpelah from Ephron the Hittite, he already gotten a toehold in the land his descendants would conquer. So he had no reason to ask for more. Then too, if he hadn't died forever somewhere between 2000 and 1500 BCE, he would have had to witness or at least hear about the horrors wreaked at his tomb in Hebron by the crazed terrorist Baruch Goldstein in 1994 (29 dead, 125 injured). Admiring fellow maniacs erected a monument to Goldstein, but it was bulldozed away. Jews have also been murdered occasionally near the Hebron site. One can't help recalling that the Latin word for sacred (*sacer*) also means "accursed," "criminal," and "wicked."

So what are we to make of Abraham's "life story," at this early stage before we examine what grew out of it? (Of course, any notion of an original core-narrative is just a manner of speaking, since the episodes comprising it undoubtedly got their final form long after they were first told, heard, and interpreted. Legends beget legends.) Most basically, this is the story of a very lucky man. He dodged dangers and conflicts, and lived happily ever after. His luck was insured by his inexplicable meetings with an invisible "God," who gave a lot and didn't ask for much in return—apart from that Binding business. What he really demanded was worship (an altar here, an animal sacrifice there)—as he would in all his future manifestations—and rejection of any third-rate alien deities. An utterly sensible *quid pro quo*, one would think. And Abraham died in bed, something not all prophets manage to do.

But in view of all the poisonous growths destined to bloom from this cycle of tales, we have to put Abraham in a harsher light and raise some skeptical questions. The first, and plainly impossible, one is: where does all this stuff come from? Somebody, it seems, we don't know who, we don't know where, told other people a bunch of stories. Or, more likely, somebody, we don't know who, we don't know where, imagined somebody else (a "prophet") telling other people some stories. Those tales made little empirical sense (nonagenarian pregnancy? a crowd of men magically struck blind? a woman turned into a block of salt?), and seemed designed to flatter the protagonist (or the protagonist's "biographer" as the bringer of such sensational news) by making him an extremely important person: the recipient of a mighty revelation from some kind of supernatural being, whatever such beings are.

The fact that this God has no clear identity might seem problematic—though his or its ability to speak the language of his or its human interlocutor is a definite plus—but monotheism has made a virtue of this near-total obscurity by stressing and glorifying the "mystery" of the Divine. Wittgenstein may have thought that when you come to a subject you can't speak of, you have to shut up; but the theologians have forged merrily ahead, as if inspired by Paul's well-known exclamation, "O the depth of the riches both of the wisdom and knowledge of God! How unsearchable are his judgments, and his ways past finding out!" (Rom. 11.33). Past finding out, but not past frenetically applauding.

True to the Pauline principle, God's behavior throughout the Abraham cycle is more or less incomprehensible. Why choose one particular man for special treatment? Why not let everyone in on the fun? Why this highly selective interference in history? What does "appear to" or "speak to" mean when the speaker has no physical components? Why is God so intent on being adored? (Does a Nobel Prize winner or an M.V.P. worry whether kids on the other side of the globe know about him?) What's going on here?

To answer—or try to get some purchase on—that question, we'll have to spend some time scanning the creeds, codes, and cults of the monotheistic religions, but even a brief consideration of the Abrahamic legends suggests some basic problems. 1) There's no reason to give any credence to these stories or to the murky deity who appears in them; 2) Nor is there any reason to trust the tellers, actual or supposed, of these tales; 3) This is true because, among other things, of the suspicious interchangeability of God and man (males) here: Initial contact between them leads man to swear loyalty to the ultra-great God (*Allahu akbar*) , which proves how great man is for having been invited to this encounter, and greater still for heaping praise on God, who, after all the flattery, is inclined to do still more favors for his creature, who naturally further exalts the deity, and so on ad infinitum. 4) Worship itself debases both the giver and the recipient (if he exists). God becomes a dipsomaniac, with man as his enabler. Worshipers resemble the courtiers of some Roman or Byzantine emperor, exhausting themselves in fulsome adulation of His Majesty. It sounds preposterously outdated, but it continues. The Jesuit order, of which this writer was a member back in the 1960's, still has its motto *Ad majorem Dei gloriam*, i.e., all hallelujahs, all the time, the Adonai Advertising Agency. Christians have taken the idea of *laus perennis* further than anyone, with contemplative orders dedicated to 24/7 praise of the Infinite Ego on High. Though mostly a Catholic affair (nuns in "perpetual adoration" of the Most Blessed Sacrament, etc.), there is also a "Neocharismatic" IHOP (International House of Prayer) in Kansas City, Missouri, where believers truckle around the clock.

We use words like "adore" or "worship" loosely; but who would want to be literally worshiped by a "lower" creature, a pigeon, say, a squirrel, or even a pet? And 5) All this intercourse with "the Holy"—in prayer, worship, sacrifice, etc.—turns out to have no immediate connection with morality. (The 613 commandments of the Law only come into focus after God has given up appearing on earth.) In fact, passion for the *mysterium tremendum et fascinans* can have deeply immoral consequences, as the pages of the Torah, Canon Law, and Sharia demonstrate. Morality or ethics is essentially rational analysis—or else God would have to send a constant stream of revelatory e-mails to earth as new moral dilemmas kept cropping up. And so you don't need God to be moral.

Monotheism, then, is background music for group aggrandizement. Alfred North Whitehead was quite wrong to say that religion is what an individual does with his solitariness—any such private devotion is a much later and less significant phase. As the Abrahamic stories indicate, religion is all about group identity and power. And you don't so much have to achieve moral goodness at this stage as conform to the customs of the tribe, e.g., by circumcising all males. Nor does one need any sort of profound understanding to qualify as good. Rabbi Hillel may have argued in *The Ethics of the Fathers* (II, 6) that "an ignoramus can't be devout," but Christian and Muslim tradition have not agreed with him. In First Corinthians Paul *boasted* about the "foolishness" of his message: "For it is written, I will destroy the wisdom of the wise, and will bring to nothing the understanding of the prudent. Where is the wise? Where is the scribe? Where is the disputer of this world? hath not God made foolish the wisdom of the world?" (1.19-20). Dummies for the deity!

So it's no accident that the most ignorant places on earth and the least educated strata of society are also the most given to religious faith. In über-pious (compared with the rest of the First World) America the National Academy of Science is overwhelmingly atheistic or agnostic, while a hundred million dolts dismiss evolution as a crackpot "theory." The most crucial fact about the Abrahamic religions is that, putting aside their venerable antiquity and esthetic splendors, they don't add up. When your traditions are founded on a series of vivid, self-serving, testosterone-soaked fantasies, the end result is bound to be irrational. And, as we scan the misty expanses of Judaism, Christianity, and Islam, we'll keep running into rapturously proclaimed and solemnly accepted absurdities. The most natural reaction to them would be to snort or laugh out loud, but we've been brought up not to. Still, one can always hope to kick bad habits.

Chapter One

A Bad Beginning

And Joshua said unto all the people, thus saith the LORD God of Israel, Your fathers dwelt on the other side of the flood in old time, even Terah, the father of Abraham, and the father of Nachor; and they served other gods. And I took your father Abraham from the other side of the flood, and led him throughout all the land of Canaan, and multiplied his seed.

—Josh. 24:2-3

"The Jews," Nietzsche wrote in *The Antichrist* (1895), "are the most remarkable people in the history of the world, because, when confronted with the question, to be or not to be, they chose to be at any cost, with a perfectly uncanny awareness. That cost was the radical falsification of all nature, or all naturalness, of all reality, of the entire inner and outer world" (24). As Walter Kaufmann first showed, Nietzsche was no anti-Semite; and his concept of Judaism as a creative falsification is not as negative as it might first seem. (Don't *all* national and cultural identities rest on contrary-to-fact fantasies?) In any event, we can apply Nietzsche's judgment to the single greatest Jewish core text, the Book of Exodus, which presents the two essential Jewish inventions, sacred history and the Law, and try to gauge the degree of creative falsification.

Genesis has always loomed larger in the western imagination (even as Abraham is the necessary beginning of monotheism); but it essentially serves as a vivid prelude to the far more important events of Exodus (the rescue from Egypt and the giving of the Law): no Exodus, no Jews. The patriarchs of Genesis live in an idealized pastoral landscape. They are wealthy chieftains, with flocks, herds, harems etc., but with no fixed residence. They wander here and there, aided at every step by their tribal god. They dream grandly of the future; but their day-to-day preoccupations revolve around wives and children, family disputes and quarrels with neighbors. They live prodigiously long lives. The aptly named Book of Genesis is, in one way or another, obsessed with baby-making, most centrally in Abraham's leap from childless graybeard to paterfamilias. He's the Proto-Patriarch, but he merely starts the ball rolling, or the nursery rocking.

The Book of Exodus gets down to business. Genesis was full of etiological myths, poetic just-so stories, only some of which relate to Israel. But by the time Exodus opens, the original population of seventy Hebrew nomads (Gen. 46.27) arriving in Egypt has swollen to a fairytale horde of perhaps 2 ½ million (extrapolating from the 600,000 men of fighting age cited in 12.37); and the fearful Egyptians attempt to launch a genocide. Practically everything in the first nineteen chapters, up till the announcement of the Law, can be written off as fiction, along with many of the events that follow; but these daring inventions help to create and explain what scholars would call *Heilsgeschichte*, salvation history, and what billions of ordinary people would think of as the most precious part of the past.

The whole saga of the escape from Egypt exudes gleeful vindictiveness. Through it all, the Pharaoh is beyond clueless. He stupidly asks the Hebrew midwives, Shiphrah and Puah (only two for such a huge group?) to murder all the newborn boys; and then appears satisfied or baffled, when they tell them they can't follow his orders because Hebrew women, unlike the obstetrically challenged Egyptians, deliver too fast for infanticide. Then the king's daughter adopts baby Moses, and so unknowingly introduces Pharaoh's worst enemy into the palace. Critics have long been intrigued by the preposterous Hebrew etymology (from *mashah,* "he draws out") used to explain Moses' obviously Egyptian name. Freud, we know, speculated that Moses was in fact an Egyptian, which would make his exploits even more darkly comic. As the Bible sees it, Egypt is outfoxed and flattened by four Hebrews, a pair of midwives and a pair of brothers (Moses and Aaron)—if they *were* brothers.

After meeting YHWH on Horeb-Sinai, Moses goes back to Egypt to unleash the ten plagues (the Bible's finest shaggy dog story). Modern readers typically complain that the sequence of Nile-into-blood, frogs, gnats, (lice?), flies, murrain, boils, hail, locusts, darkness, and the death of the firstborn is unfair: Since God has pre-hardened Pharaoh's heart, there's no point in cruelly upping the ante, because God has also prevented him from ever wising up.

But if Pharaoh *had* shown any common sense (or pity for his subjects), that would have ruined the story. The whole idea is to pile on sadistic details and create a thunderous finish: God did what?! And he still didn't get it?! Another plague—and he STILL didn't get it?! You've GOT to be kidding! We already know how dumb the goyim can be (Esau selling his inheritance for some red pottage), but this takes the cake. No wonder the Egyptians "lent" the departing Israelites all their finest jewelry (12.35-36). Modern readers are also likely to protest about the Egyptians' being punished for the king's misdeeds (which even he wasn't responsible for).

There's no way around this issue, especially in view of the wipe-out in Chapter 14—unless perhaps one equates the malefactors with the entire population ("and the Egyptians made the children to Israel to serve with rigor. And they made their lives bitter with bondage," 1.13-14). Or maybe the bloodthirsty royal command, "And Pharaoh charged all his people, saying, Every son that is born ye shall cast into the river" (1.22), *was* carried out, though the text doesn't say so.

No matter. Despite the vast and splotchy spectrum of mostly middling human beings, the Us/Them dichotomy is firmly installed at the heart of monotheism. The prophets Jeremiah and Ezekiel would later insist on personal, not corporate guilt or innocence; and Jesus would stress the savability of lost sheep. But the binary model would always dominate: righteous/ wicked; thou shalt/thou shalt not; kosher/tref; halal/haram; saved/ damned; sheep/ goats; believer/ unbeliever; angels/ demons; heaven/hell; and, naturally, Jew/ Gentile; Christian/non-Christian; Muslim/infidel. And so on: monotheism puts the seal of divine approval on a primordial, universal (?), binary way of thinking. Ecumenists may sing paeans to dialogue; but the prophetic religions are all competing over who has the best prophet. And the greatness of the prophet reflects the greatness of his followers.

But back to the plagues of Egypt and the exodus, where we find the usual dynamic of melodrama at work: While it's delicious to rejoice over the escape from slavery and the annihilation of the oppressors, it's their cruelty and especially Pharaoh's hard-heartedness that make the whole adventure tick. What a bore if the Israelites had simply strolled out of Egypt and queued up for the ferry across the Red (or Reed) Sea. The *Schadenfreude* wouldn't have been complete without the slaughter of the firstborn (*all* the first born, human and bovine) and the mass drowning of Pharaoh's cavalry. It's good guys vs. bad guys: monotheism ultimately has no truck with tragedy, because people are either good or bad, the Bible doesn't deal with tragic flaws (except, perhaps in the case of Saul), the Almighty Judge in charge of everything is never less than perfectly just, and hence his outcomes leave nothing to be desired. No appeals can filed after Doomsday.

So the villainy of the Egyptians was indispensable in making the Israelites who they were (even as Christians needed the catastrophe of Jesus' crucifixion, engineered jointly, the Gospels tell us, by Roman and Jewish leaders, to become the Church). That's why the Bible claims that the entire population of Israel left Egypt under Moses' guidance and entered Canaan under Joshua's guidance (though these were completely different generations). Modern biblical scholars who are also liberal believers acknowledge both that Exodus' numbers are inflated (how could such a mass of humanity have survived in the deserts of the Sinai?) and that there probably were some other Hebrews, for example around Shechem, who never went to Egypt and who would thus have met their invading kinsmen in Canaan.

But the important thing, such critics argue, isn't the number of people involved in this slave revolt, but the fact that it actually happened, in some form or other. So what if the body of water crossed was a lake full of reeds rather than a full-fledged sea? So what if there was no Cecil B. DeMille moment with towering walls of water intersected by a paved superhighway? What counts is that a group of people felt they had been liberated by a Transcendent Power, and that this liberation created their identity. And not only had this really taken place, it could be relived through the magic of sacred memory. As the Passover seder says, "In every generation let each man look on himself as if *he* came forth out of Egypt. As it is said: 'And thou shalt tell thy son in that day, saying: It is because of that which the Lord did for me when I came forth out of Egypt' [Ex. 13:8]. It was not only our fathers that the Holy One, blessed be he, redeemed, but us as well did he redeem along with them. As it is said: 'And he brought us out from thence, that he might bring us in, to give us the land which he swore unto our fathers'" [Deut. 6.23], *The Schocken Passover Seder*, p. 59.

This is the essence of "sacred history": God intervenes in human life, usually to help, but sometimes to punish (tough love) a group of his favorite friends. And these world-changing events don't simply occur and then fade away; they are kept alive by—and in turn help to keep alive—the group remembering them. Among the most familiar later examples of this are the Eucharist and the hajj. God brings back the past and lets you relive the highlights.

Sacred history is the key to monotheism, but it's false through and through. The exodus never took place, any more than Jesus' resurrection or Muhammad's night journey. The reasons for this are all well known and well rehearsed (e.g., it is mentioned nowhere outside the Bible); but, amazingly, they have yet to penetrate the hardened skulls of nearly half the planet's population. There were and are no reliable witnesses to any of the supposed events, which violate the laws of nature, something that has never been reliably attested to by anyone at any time in any place. Miracles always occur in the subterranean depths of the past, never in the well-lit labs, lecture halls, or town squares of the faithless present. And, as David Hume argues, a claim has yet to be put forth for any miracle where the probability of its being true would outweigh the likelihood that the reporters were mistaken or just making it up.

Cherchez l'homme. No miracle was ever unwelcome to the person telling about it or to the group he represents. And among the most suspicious qualities of this totally suspect genre is the way the stories always work out to the advantage of the miracle-reporter's tribe and audience. Miracles are so *convenient.* But then, of course, they stop. In *The Disappearance of God* (1995) Richard Elliott Friedman traces the stages of God's exit: the last person God personally appears to in the Old Testament is Solomon (who lived almost a millennium before the Christian era). The last public miracle God performs is the sending down of fire from heaven to consume Elijah's sacrifice in the contest with the prophets of Baal on Mount Carmel (ca. 860 BCE). His last "private miracle" comes when he reverses the shadow on the sundial for King Hezekiah, thereby granting him an extra fifteen years of life (this was more than 700 years before the time of Christ). Thereafter, some prophets will maintain that God has spoken to them; but eventually that ends too, the canon closes, and believers have only the Tanakh and the Talmud to figure things out for themselves. It was great while it lasted, but the monotheists all confess that at some point Revelation dries up.

But unlike Christians and Muslims, the Jews weren't blessed with a long string of political, military, and propaganda victories to foster the myth of a God who had specially selected and protected them. The centuries of travail and slaughter, culminating in the Holocaust, would seem to expose that myth as a fraud, as well as validate Nietzsche's view of the Jews as engaging in heroic falsification (choosing to be their mythic selves instead of assimilating into some larger, safer ethnic mass and thus becoming happily anonymous). But if Nietzsche were alive today, he'd have to add a footnote to acknowledge how many Jews in the wake of the Holocaust *have* in one way or another rejected their classic identity, for example along the lines of Kadya Molodovsky (d. 1974) who in "God of Mercy" bitterly turns away from the whole notion of chosenness.

> God of mercy,
> Choose another people,
> for a while.
> We're tired of dying and death.
> We've no more prayers left.
> Choose another people
> for a while.
> We've no more blood
> in our veins to sacrifice.
> Our house has become a desert,

> without enough ground to dig graves in.
> No more lamentations,
> no more songs of woe
> in our old books.

(It may be illogical to invoke a God only to curse him, but that turns out to be one of the deity's most useful features.) Whether through downright atheism (Primo Levi, etc.), or the replacement of Judaism with edgy secular Yiddishkeit (Philip Roth), or the timeworn path of exogamy (Jewish Hollywood), Jews have found a whole array of routes to disidentification.

But the long and short of sacred history is that it's bogus. Miracles don't happen, can't happen; and so won't happen. God has abandoned his people—not that he ever existed or actively cherished them; but in the sense that it used to be possible for thinking people to believe that he did. Now, not so much. Nobody's history is sacred (penetrated by supernatural forces). The Jews half-admitted this when they began to dream about the Messiah and an apocalyptic scenario for the End of Days—two *Deus ex machina* solutions to the increasingly desperate state of Jewish life. History turned out to be a dead end; and the only conceivable way out was for God and his superhuman agents to make an emergency landing on planet earth to put the whole mess out of its misery. And any day now ...

Such dreams inevitably called for bloody wipe-outs of Israel's tormentors (see Isaiah 24-27), a theme borrowed by Christians and Muslims in their own frenzied, vengeful scripts for the Last Judgment. All such comforting (for the "just") visions defy refutation because, as Freud pointed out in *The Future of an Illusion* (1927), unhappy believers can always hope that although the longed for, Godot-like Savior/Redeemer never comes today, he (no women need apply) might just be coming tomorrow or the day after. You never can tell.

Of course, with the passage of time such hopes, logically speaking, dissolve like shadows at nightfall. One of the main reasons why the chances of escaping what James Joyce called the nightmare of history look so slim to fair-minded Bible readers is that Israelite and Jewish writers are so unremittingly negative in describing that nightmare. From the patriarchs to the exodus to the judges and kings until the virtual end of national autonomy in the Babylonian Exile (a period of perhaps 1,200 years), both the leaders of the people and the hoi polloi are described, for the most part, as abject failures.

From the ethnic cleansing of Shechem by Simeon and Levi (Gen. 34) to the depredations of evil kings like Menachem (745-738 BCE), whose specialty was disemboweling pregnant women, the Bible's history of Israel would make the most besotted patriot weep. The absolute nadir may have been the civil war against the Benjaminites in Judges 20-21. The horror begins with a gang rape that closely copies that of the Sodomites (except that it succeeds) and ends with the slaughter of something over 90,000 men AND the massacre of men, women, and children from Jabesh-gilead for not joining the campaign against Benjamin. So much blood flows all over the whole episode that the concluding scene, the abduction and rape of the virgins of Shiloh, seems like a sort of merry satyr play. The numbers are grotesquely inflated; and we have no idea of what facts, if any, lie at the heart of this lunatic war story. But the dismay and national shame it conjures up are unmistakable: not just Israel behaving badly, but Israel behaving worse than the worst of the gentiles. God might well wonder why he ever wasted his time on such losers.

Whatever their motive, the authors, whoever they were, of these tales of failure provide devastating ammunition against the whole notion of sacred history; but that's their problem. The widespread scholarly assumption that the key texts of the Bible were collected and edited in the wake of the catastrophic downfall of the southern kingdom of Judah in 586 BCE might well explain their recurrent notes of anger and disgust. Where did we go wrong, one imagines the collators wondering as they sifted through the ruins of their once promising history. Godless modem readers are liable to find such vehement self-criticism refreshing, especially when compared with the triumphalism of the New Testament and the Qur'an, where the bad guys are always the other guys.

Call it what you will, frankness, obsessive critical scrutiny, or just a willingness to wash dirty cultural linen in public, this should come as no surprise, given the rocky start that *Heilsgeschichte* got in the none-too-edifying behavior of Abraham, who was no saint. For all that, Abraham (and all the other imperfect interlocutors with God who followed him) did believe the primordial delusion that they were interacting with some enormous-but-personal cosmic entity. Or at least the narrators of these encounters believed it. And even if no great cult of the personality has surrounded the first prophet, Abraham, like the one (minus images) that has attached itself to the "last:" of the prophets, Muhammad, we're dealing with the same brand of self-deception.

So what was the prophetic experience (since it certainly wasn't deliberate fraud, except maybe with Joseph Smith)? Hallucinations? Reveries? Schizophrenic disorders? (See the Conclusion.) Something provoked by a mid-life crisis? Since practically all prophets are male, might their altered states of consciousness point to the seldom studied malaise of uterus-envy, a longing compounded of heightened awareness of mortality and frustration at the inability to give birth? The prophet has substitute-children in the form of disciples and followers, with the prospect of defeating death through a message that will last far longer than his own brief span. That message comes from his innards, the fruit of "intercourse" with the deity (where God plays the male role and the prophet that of the receptive female). "Bearing" it is often a painful—sometimes even life-threatening—process, and seems to prompt a tender, maternal concern for the miraculous (like all babies) message.

One final argument for the falsity of the prophetic experience: it can't be repeated by others, except in the palest way. (If it could, everyone would be a prophet.) Generations of devotees sit at the metaphorical feet of the prophets, reading, memorizing, and meditating on the sacred texts. Some may feel an auto-erotic jolt of sorts, but never the same grand, tumultuous epiphany. (It would be arrogant and disrespectful to lay claim to an equal experience anyway.) A scientist can repeat what other scientists have done (and correct their findings). A performer can "copy" (in various ways) another's work of art; but prophetic meetings with the Almighty are one-off moments, unrepeatable because they never happened and couldn't happen, at least as described. Three visitors don't morph into one. Fire and sulfur don't pour out of the sky when an omnipotent Spook becomes righteously indignant. Burning bushes get quickly incinerated. And so forth. Everyone knows that; but billions of people are willing to blink such absurdities when there's the equivalent of organ music playing in the background.

Of course, only theological hard-liners would have us believe that the miraculous doings in the Bible are factually true. You can't argue with Voltaire that the chronology of Abraham's life is a joke. E.g., the transition from Gen. 11.31 to 12.1 makes Abram at least 130 years old when he left Haran. Liberal commentators, by contrast, are willing to write off most of the razzle-dazzle episodes as figurative or fanciful in one way or another. The texts themselves speak of "signs" (divine power dramatically manifested) rather than "miracles"—the latter assumes the suspension or violation of nature's otherwise unchanging laws, which the ancient Israelites didn't recognize. Hence, many scriptural experts will concede that a camcorder at the site of the *magnalia Dei* recounted in both Testaments would not have captured the sights and sounds that believers have always loved to imagine: YHWH thundering on

Mount Sinai, Jesus bursting forth from the tomb, the angel Jibril swooping down from heaven to reveal the Qur'an to Muhammad on the Laylat al-Qadr (night of destiny).

But at a minimum, pious demythologizers will insist, real *psychic* events were taking place, real contact was being made between the original witness (whether a concrete individual or a symbolic stand-in for the community) and the Most High-Eternal One-Ground of Being-and so forth. At this point, however, the borderline between history and make-believe begins to dim and blur. The crucial question here is: how many worlds are there? For secular moderns there's only one; for monotheists there's that mysterious extra dimension, the divine, that wraps us round while mostly hiding itself, except for rare flamboyant incursions into the olive-drab, quotidian sphere.

But here, if anywhere, the burden of proof is on the affirmative. Reaching back to a host of disparate, distinguished figures, from Epicurus to Ockham to Laplace to Darwin, non spiritualists have seen no need to posit purely hypothetical entities to describe and help us navigate the universe. Experience, not old husbands' tales, is our guide. It makes much more sense to assume that the amazing theophanies attributed to Abraham and his descendants are aberrant phantasmagoria, which breaks down and evaporates in the bright light of day. Sacred history is non-history. And we're still stuck in our old mortal skins, as shown by the utter failure of Abraham & Co. to tell us anything credible about the deity who bumped into them.

Biblical "history" leads to Law. Although God made covenants with Adam, Noah, and Abraham, he didn't get serious about legal obligations till Moses. Adam was told to increase and multiply (no problem!), while keeping his hand off the fruit of the tree of knowledge (God likes his children to stay infantile). Noah was told to get on with the increasing and multiplying, now that God had reduced the world's entire human population to eight after the Flood, as well as not to commit murder and (proleptically) to kosher all his meat. Abraham had to worship YHWH alone, circumcise all males, and then pass the worse-than-idiotic sacrifice-test. But, starting with Moses, things were going to get a lot more complicated and demanding.

Just about everyone admits that laws develop over time: evolve, alter, get replaced, etc. So the idea that God could deposit the entire Torah on earth in a single, glossy package is ipso facto absurd. But, if one ignores this and other pragmatic difficulties (why were laws concerning settled urban life issued while the Israelites still had years and years of roaming in the wilderness ahead of them?), the belief that morality is, in various senses, divine has to be rated one of the most widespread, popular convictions/delusions of all time. The commandments, whether the Top Ten or all 613 *mitvot*, come from God and lead us to God, or so they say. Keeping the Sabbath, for example, imitates God's resting on the seventh day, and makes us, in some unspeakable fashion, *like him* (which isn't as grand as it sounds, if we consider that, as a projection of ourselves, God was always very much *like us*).

As we've seen, there's a subversive element in all this, namely that once God leaves the Israelites (us) with a more or less complete book of instructions for how to behave, we really don't need him anymore. And with the death of Moses, God starts making himself scarce until for all practical purposes he vanishes. The supreme (male) human task then becomes studying the Torah, which, done properly, absorbs an adult man's every waking moment (his wife can multitask to support his sacred scholarship). So long as one accepts the Law as divine, then, God has not disappeared; he's just continuing his presence in a different, though much less sexy, fashion.

But, for all sorts of reasons, this will never do. First, all laws in history have always been human products, with human limitations and crudities. They're deeply marked by the circumstances they arise in. How could it be otherwise? Alternately, if there were a God, all-wise but a pure Spirit, how could he legislate for humans, having not the faintest existential notion of what embodied life was like? Second, what exactly would the religious-sacred component of laws come down to? And why would we need any such component? Well, it could make all offenses worse by calling them crimes against God.

But then why should a perfect and perfectly happy being mind what his ant-like creatures do to one another? Or why should he be riled by "personal" insults directed against him, by blasphemers, say? Then again, the religious element here might be the liability to eternal, extraterrestrial reward and punishment, depending on one's "final grade" upon exiting life. But one look at the Beyond as sketched in Christian and Muslim holy books is enough, as we'll see, to make readers snort with laughter. "He will reward them [the blessed] for their steadfastness with Paradise and robes of silk. Reclining there upon soft couches, they shall feel neither the scorching heat nor the biting cold ... They shall be served on silver dishes, and beakers as large as goblets; silver goblets which they themselves shall measure: and cups brim-full with ginger-flavoured water from a fount called Salsabil. [What? That's *it*?] They shall be attended by boys graced with eternal youth, who to the beholder's eyes will seem like sprinkled pearls" (76:11-19). Christian heaven is far worse, a dull diorama of palm-waving North-Korean-style choristers hailing the Dear Leader day and night. The Jewish folklore about a giant banquet of steaks from Leviathan and the Wild Ox might be good for a few hours, though not much longer and never for vegetarians.

Another mode, at once the most pragmatic and the most preposterous, of understanding divine law is the Bible's constant assertion (in the Deuteronomic Principle) that obedience to divine law guarantees prosperity while disobedience brings disaster. But this is such a stretch that the Bible itself, e.g., in Jeremiah 12.1-2, Job

21.7-26, Ecclesiastes 4.1-2, etc. occasionally denies or questions it. And it's to the great credit of Rabbi Yannai in *Pirke Abot,* IV, 19 (ca. 200 CE), that he said it was beyond any human power to explain why the wicked prosper and the righteous suffer. Purists might object that if the D.P. really worked, then morality would simply be a series of earned pay-offs; and virtuous people would be coupon-clippers. But not to worry, the quickest glance out the window will establish how often good behavior is not rewarded and bad behavior is. You can't get more self-evident than that. When in trouble, call 911, not God.

But, beyond these philosophical objections, the most obvious complaint against supposedly divine laws is the sheer number of them that are wrong or stupid or both. Sharia provides more up-to-date examples of this than the Torah, most of whose provisions have long lapsed into dead letter; but for sheer gaudy nonsense the Law of Moses is unmatched. Where to begin? The laws against idolatry, culminating in the *herem*, or ban, which calls for the absolute, merciless destruction of pagan peoples (Deut. 7.1-2, etc.) are patently the worst, as seen in the annihilation of Jericho. Fortunately, this blood-curdling command, along with the related order to kill every prophet, diviner, or family member promoting the worship of anybody but Yahweh (Deut. 13), was in all likelihood never carried out, and most assuredly not on the scale depicted in the Book of Joshua.

But it's the thought that counts. (We know what Catholics have done to heretics and Muslims do to apostates.) And all the specifically religious dictates of the Law turn out to be severely problematical. The office of priest is reserved to—duh—men. The dopey, elaborate sacrifices needlessly inflict pain and misery on animals (like the scapegoat driven into the wilderness as an offering to the non-existent demon Azazel [Lev. 16.10]. The endless dietary laws of *kashrut* are an exercise in futility, made worse, again, by the divine encouragement given to animal slaughter and meat-consumption.

Menstruation is dirty and disgusting (Lev. 15.19-24). "And if a woman have an issue, and her issue in her flesh be blood, she shall be put apart seven days: and whosoever toucheth her shall be unclean until the even. And everything that she lieth upon in her separation shall be unclean: everything also that she sitteth upon shall be unclean. And whosoever toucheth her bed shall wash his clothes, and bathe himself in water, and be unclean until the even." Isaiah has few terms viler than "menstruous cloth" (30.22), alternately "dirty rag," 64.6), echoed in the "menstruous woman" of Lamentations 1.17.

"But that's only logical, given the consistently second-class status of women in the Torah (and Christianity and Islam). A woman who is found lacking an intact hymen on her wedding night is condemned to be stoned to death (for "playing the whore in her father's house," Deut. 22.20, since of course he's in charge of her body). Wives suspected of infidelity can be forced to take the terrifying "water of bitterness" trial (Num. 5); but there's no test for cheating husbands. You might, if you were on drugs, call God the author of such legislation; but it sounds more like the savage whims of jealous, possessive men. Naturally enough, the state of Israel pays no attention to such poisonous nonsense in its civil or criminal code.

Another noxious element in the Torah is its lavish application of the death penalty. Regardless of whether such laws were ever implemented, they must have helped to promote the cult of capital punishment that prevailed in many "Christian" countries till the late 20th century, and is still both practiced and highly praised in the truly benighted USA. According to the Bible, capital punishment is prescribed for a wide variety of offenses (apart from idolatry), such as breaking the Sabbath (Ex. 31.14, Num. 15.32-36), witchcraft (Ex. 22.18, which proved handy in Christian times), adultery (Deut.

22.22), bestiality (Ex. 22.19), rape (Deut, 22.25), kidnapping (Deut. 24.7), blasphemy (Lev. 23.14) , gay sex (Lev. 20.13), striking or cursing one's parents (Ex. 21.15,17), sleeping with someone else's fiancée (Deut. 22.23-24), and being a drunken and disorderly son (Deut. 21.18-21)—among others. God is a truly lousy legislator, though we have only the babblings of his prophetic law clerks to evaluate him by.

The obvious "naïve" (i.e., rational) question here is: Did we really need God to tell us all this? What exactly is the element of divine wisdom in the provisions permitting slavery (Ex. 21. 12, etc.)? How could God be so crude and cruel as to say—or to let writers quote him as saying—that there was no penalty for killing a slave if he or she survives at least a day or after being mistreated, because "the slave is his money" (Ex. 21.21)? What is the religious feature of the right accorded any male Israelite of "marrying" any captive slave girl who turns him on (Deut. 21.10-13)? Thanks to Islam, heavenly permission, if not encouragement, to take more than one wife (Deut. 21.15), now seems less outrageous than it might, but why did YHWH single out the sluttish daughters of priests for burning to death (Lev. 21.9), instead of, say, stoning? With all the other misogynistic laws in place, why the extra provision for cutting off the hand of a woman who helps her husband in a fight by grabbing his opponent's genitals (Lev. 25.12)? Yahweh thinks of everything.

What of all the silly, though non-lethal, legislation that, for example, bans cross-dressing (Deut. 22.5—that helped to seal Joan of Arc's fate), wearing mixed fabrics (Deut. 22.11), plowing with an ox and an ass together (Deut. 22.10), or sowing vineyards with two kinds of seed (Deut. 22.2)? What of the deadly boring instructions about the ark of the testimony, the lamp and the lamp stands, the curtains and frames for the tabernacle, the veil, the altar of acacia wood, the holy garments, ephod, and breastplate for Aaron, the outfits for Aaron's sons, the consecration ceremony, the altar of incense and all that liturgical jazz (Ex. 25-30) ? Why did God bother with his long account of the furnishings of the sanctuary in Ex. 36-39, the mumbo-jumbo about skin diseases, leprosy, bodily emissions, and whatnot (Lev. 13-15)?

Actually, the reason behind all this seems clear enough—a fanatical quest for ritual "purity," which probably required all the witch-doctor details. For instance, in Lev. 14. 48-56 (settle back and enjoy one of the least-read portions of the Bible): "And if the priest shall come in [to a house with a "leprous mold" on the walls], and look upon it, and behold, the plague hath not spread in the house, after the house was plastered, then the priest shall pronounce the house clean, because the plague is healed, And he shall take to cleanse the house two birds, and cedar wood, and scarlet, and hyssop. And he shall kill one of the birds in an earthen vessel over running water. And he shall take the cedar wood, and the hyssop, and the scarlet, and the living bird, and dip them in the blood of the slain bird, and in the running water, and sprinkle the house seven times. And he shall cleanse the house with the blood of the bird, and with the running water, and with the living bird, and with the hyssop, and with the scarlet. But he shall let go the living bird out of the city into the open fields, and make the atonement for the house, and it shall be clean." Liberal commentators dismiss such anthropological curiosities as irrelevant; but if Revelation is in any sense a package deal, why shouldn't this passage be granted as much respect as, say, Moses' face shining with the presence of God as he descended Mount Sinai (Ex. 34.29), or any other verse of the Hummash (Lev. 11.16, say, which bans eating sea gulls)? Divine law is divine law.

And then there's the notorious rule of the talion (Ex. 21. 23-2; Lev. 24.20). Devout biblicists hasten to add that "an eye for an eye" is meant to keep legal vengeance within limits, as opposed to the overkill that one sees so often, for example, in reprisals for partisan attacks. Fair enough, but the principle hardly qualifies as enlightened: which is why "truth and reconciliation" committees have wisely dispensed with it. After all, as many people have observed, one doesn't rape rapists or burn down the houses of arsonists. And what is the purpose of vengeance anyway, except to satisfy uncontrollable human emotions?

One is glad to report that not all the Omniscient One's ethical communiqués are evil, excessive, pointless, or tedious. There *are* flashes of humanity, restraint, and even kindness in the Torah. The Israelites are told not to wrong or oppress strangers, orphans, or widows, since *they* were once strangers in the land of Egypt (Ex. 22.21). In fact, this commandment is so serious that God threatens to kill anyone who violates it. Every now and then the Bible calls for "humane" treatment of animals, e.g., one has to release the mother bird when one takes her eggs or nestlings (Deut. 22.6-7); the Israelites are not supposed to cut down fruit trees growing near a city they are besieging (Deut. 20.19-20), and so forth. Domestic animals (perforce) get to enjoy the Sabbath (Deut. 5.14), which is clearly one of Scripture's most sensible ideas.

Though the Old Testament is generally much more practical than the New Testament, there are two famous utopian provisions in the Law: the sabbatical year (Lev. 25. 2-1; Deut. 15.1-3) and the jubilee (Lev. 25.8-17). No society could ever come to such beatific screeching halts for an entire year; but there's a strain of noble idealism in imagining that it could: "You shall not sow your field, or prune your vineyard. What grows of itself in your harvest you shall not reap, the grapes of your undressed vine you shall not gather: it shall be year of solemn rest for the land. The sabbath of the land shall provide food for you; for yourself, and for your male and female slaves, and for your hired servant and the sojourner who lives with you; for your cattle also and for the beasts that are in your land all its yield shall be for food" (RSV). Another grand ethical concept that's not exactly utopian, but perhaps too broadly framed is "Thou shalt not follow a multitude to do evil" (Ex. 23.1), which could have turned the 20th century around if more people had paid attention to it.

In transmitting the Torah, then, Yahweh had his good days and his bad days; but the end result hardly seems to justify the millennial obsessive-compulsive cult that Jews have devoted to it. Of course in modern times the finest Jewish minds have, by a wide margin, turned to secular law and ethics. To put it bluntly, even if we assume (but why should we?) that God gave the whole moral enterprise an initial impulse, before taking French leave, now that he's gone silent, we can obviously do a much better job than he ever did. The history that his covenant supposedly developed out of and was based on is false. The laws he supposedly gave, or were invented in his name, are an ugly patchwork and by now beyond repair. The fables about Abraham gave rise to an unbelievable series of hypertrophied dreams and delusions. Judaism has had its day and should by rights disappear. The Jews, one hopes, we will always have with us.

In any event, the story of Abraham can readily serve, as it was no doubt intended to, as the distilled essence of Jewish henotheism—later tidied up into monotheism. At its heart is no abstract philosophical argument (and one could speculate that later attempts to "justify" religion rationally were a sure sign that it was ailing), but the breathtaking claim that a (literally) unspeakable Energy had invaded the space called Israel. And this gave rise to the paradox of unearned chosenness: God's visitations cause and attest to Abraham's unique stature, but he and his descendants aren't supposed to boast about it. Moses warns them in Deuteronomy that although, "the LORD thy God hath chosen thee to be a special people unto himself, above all people that are upon the face of the earth, the LORD did not set his love upon you, because ye were more in number than any people (for you were the fewest of all people), but because the LORD loved you, and because he would keep the oath which he had sworn unto thy fathers ..." (7.6-8).

As the Israelites prepare to invade Canaan, to finally cash in on God's promise to Abraham, Moses, the greatest of the Hebrew prophets, wants to make sure that they don't take any credit for the coming victories: "Not for thy righteousness, or for the uprightness of thy heart, dost thou go to possess their land: but for the wickedness of these nations the LORD doth drive them out before thee. And that he may perform the word which the LORD swore unto thy fathers, Abraham, Isaac, and Jacob" (9.5). Israel, he says, is a "stiffnecked people" (9.7)—as Moses knew better than anyone—and they better not forget it. Compared with Muhammad's constant flattery of "true believers" (e.g., "You are the noblest community ever raised up for mankind. You enjoin justice and forbid Evil" 3:110), the Bible's persistent criticism of Israel comes as a relief, even if it's also reminiscent of an OCD.

This peculiar status is at once private and public, private in the sense that all crucial communications between God and his prophets take place *entre quatre yeux* (assuming the deity has two eyes), and so we always have to take somebody else's word for it, and public in the sense that the supposed interchanges are forever repeated in liturgical rehearsals and readings, where they take on a proverbial life of their own. Such ceremonies enable Jews to re-experience the Covenant, and they create a culture that separates bonded members from outsiders. A whole panoply of customs—circumcision, dietary laws, use of a "sacred" language, clothing, marriage restrictions, etc.—isolates the community in a highly concrete "specialness"—as happens with many Muslims and, to a lesser extent, Christians. Sometimes this leads –how not?—to a laughable parochialism, as we read in *Everyman's Talmud* (1949), where Abraham Cohen cites three bits of rabbinical piety: "'Among those who will inherit the World to Come are: who resides in the land of Israel and who rears his soul in the study of the Torah' (Pes. 113a). 'Whoever walks a distance of four cubits in the land of Israel is assured of being a son of the World to Come' (Keth. 111a). 'He who studies the laws of Judaism is assured of being a son of the World to Come' (Meg. 28b).'' "HE who," of course.

These communities can become intense mini-worlds, where the individual is free to immerse and lose himself (again it's mostly men who do this), as anyone who has spent some time in a yeshivah, seminary, monastery, or madrasa can attest. Membership in the congregation of a synagogue, church, or mosque provides a generally much thinner version of the same all-engulfing religious sensation. This pattern of narrowing and intensifying should come as no surprise, since any person so inclined can find something similarly hallucinogenic in the mini-worlds of alcohol, cocaine, crystal meth, gambling, or unsafe sex, among others.

But unlike those addictions, religious fervor carries no social stigma, quite the contrary. Praised for their monomaniacal habit, monotheists have the often undeserved reputation of moral uprightness, especially when such uprightness is defined in creedal terms. Thus among extremely conservative religious groups, crimes like shooting Arabs, shooting abortion-providers, or shooting one's wayward daughters can be viewed as signs of extraordinary virtue. But religious passion has no right to the privileged status that it enjoys among both conventional dullards and politically correct academics, like the oft-quoted Prof. John Esposito of Georgetown and other Religious Studies mavens. Monotheism began as nonsense and has continued as nonsense. The Jews invented it and passed it on to Christians and Muslims, though often without the sternly self-critical element of Judaism. Abraham was no hero—and never claimed to be one; but Jesus is presented from the start, and often presents himself, as a superhero ("Heaven and earth shall pass away, but my words shall not pass away," Mk. 13.31); and Muhammad, if you can believe him and his followers, was something like the greatest man who ever lived (hence, "the man who defies God and His apostle shall abide forever in the fire of hell," 9.:63).Monotheism starts off badly and only gets worse.

Chapter Two

The Son Who *Was* Sacrificed

Then answered the Jews, and said unto him, Say we not well that thou art a Samaritan, and hast a devil? Jesus answered, I have not a devil; but I honour my Father, and ye do dishonour me. And I seek not mine own glory: there is one that seeketh and judgeth. Verily, verily, I say unto you, If a man keep my saying, he shall never see death. Then said the Jews unto him, Now we know that thou hast a devil. Abraham is dead, and the prophets; and thou sayest, If a man keep my saying, he shall never taste of death. Art thou greater than our father Abraham, which is dead? and the prophets are dead: whom makest thou thyself? Jesus answered, If I honour myself, my honour is nothing: it is my Father that honoureth me; of whom ye say, that he is your God: Yet ye have not known him; but I know him: and if I should say, I know him not, I shall be a liar like unto you: but I know him, and keep his saying. Your father Abraham rejoiced to see my day: and he saw [it], and was glad. Then said the Jews unto him, Thou art not yet fifty years old, and hast thou seen Abraham? Jesus said unto them, Verily, verily, I say unto you, Before Abraham was, I am.

—John 8.48-58

The central irony—and foundational metaphor—of Christianity is its failure-based success. If Jesus and his early disciples had gotten a warmer reception from their Jewish audience, and if the Romans hadn't crucified him, the fiery prophet from Nazareth would never have become the divine figure worshiped by gentiles and a relative handful of renegade Jews. The joke about death as a smart career move is a tired one, but imagine Jesus living to a ripe old age. He undoubtedly would have cut back on his apocalyptic intensity and softened some of his radical positions (or overheated language), like suggesting that men make themselves eunuchs for the Kingdom of Heaven (Mt. 19.12) or to give up everything and follow him (Mk. 10.21), or not to worry about what they were going to eat, drink, or wear (Mt. 6.31), etc. And it would have been harder to divinize a middle-aged Jesus who had married and settled down, much less a decrepit, white-bearded one turned cranky and forgetful.

But Jesus disappeared after a public life of at most three years (John) or perhaps just one (Synoptics), which left the Evangelists free—writing a generation or two after his death—to improvise and shape his life as they, and their community, wished. They could exalt him and make him say things that no Jew would have dreamed of saying (like "Before Abraham was, I am"), and they could turn his life into a perfect recapitulation and fulfillment of Jewish history. Instead of abandoning their rich, dense tradition, they could and did hijack it and take it to places it was never meant to go. Then they radically simplified the complex, burdensome Law; and Christianity was ready to take the world by storm.

Much of this process involved what we would nowadays have to call invention and falsification; but it was esthetically effective, easy to picture (if not to comprehend), and psychologically liberating. Matthew's and Luke's fanciful genealogies establish Jesus as the heir to David's crown. (Since he was a Jew, he could, like all "full-blooded" Jews, trace his *yikhus* back to Abraham [Mt. 1.1; Lk. 3.34].) Their fairy tales about the virgin birth, although they disconnect him from David, Abraham, and the human race in general by denying Joseph's real fatherhood, link him to the divinely masterminded, improbable births of Isaac, Jacob and Esau, Joseph, Samson, and Samuel. Of course, Jesus would out-Isaac Isaac by an actual auto-immolation carried through to the bitter end.

Jesus' life keeps intersecting with prior sacred history. His birth is (erroneously) said to have been predicted by Isaiah (7.14). Like Moses, he escapes the Pharaoh's (Herod's) murderous plots, paradoxically going down into Egypt to do so. Like Moses, he fasts for forty days and forty nights (Ex. 34.28). Like Moses, he lays down the New Covenant in grand speeches reminiscent of Deuteronomy. He works miracles like Elijah and Elisha, multiplying food supplies (1 Kings 17.14-16; 2 Kings 4.42-44), resurrecting dead children (1 Kings 17.17-24; 2 Kings 4.32-37); healing lepers (2 Kings 5.9-14), walking on water (2 Kings 2.8), and ascending into heaven (2 Kings 2.11). Returning the favor, Elijah and Moses make a crucial cameo appearance with Jesus in the Transfiguration (Mt. 17.1-8) to put the Scriptural stamp of approval on him.

Jesus constantly quotes from the Tanakh. He uses three texts from Deuteronomy (8.3, 6.16, and 6. 13) to rout Satan when he tempts Jesus in the wilderness. He borrows from Moses' blessing in Deut. 28.3-6 to formulate the Beatitudes. He reviews various commandments in the Sermon on the Mount, not to reject them but to make them broader—and harder. He cites Hosea 6.6 to explain why he hangs around with "tax collectors and sinners." He chooses twelve disciples to symbolize the twelve tribes of Israel. He compares himself to Jonah (belly of the whale=the tomb). He often (in Matthew anyway) speaks slightingly of Gentiles. He makes a messianic entrance into Jerusalem and holds a Passover Seder (Synoptics), where he presents himself as the Paschal lamb. And he's put to death for claiming to be who he actually is, the King of Israel.

Whether he ever said, meant, or did any of these things, Jesus appears as an ultra-Jewish figure; and it's likely that at least some Jews would have revered him as a romantic rebel against religious business-as-usual, if Christians hadn't been so quick to turn him into a lethal weapon against them. Of course, remarks like the ones he is quoted making in our Johannine epigraph would have gotten him banned from the community even faster than Uriel da Costa or Spinoza. From there to the theandric Savior-Redeemer *il n'y a qu'un pas*. On the other hand, John's Gospel (4:22) does have him telling the Samaritan woman, "Salvation is from the Jews." Jesus, as the Fathers of the Church and a million other preachers have insisted, is Israelite/Jewish salvation history recalled, revived, and completed.

Historically speaking, the problem of what Jesus thought of himself is insoluble. When the rich young man asked him, "Good Master, what shall I do that I may inherit eternal life?" Jesus famously objected, "Why callest thou me good? There is no man good but one, that is, God" (Mk. 10.17-18), a line no rabbi could find fault with. The Sermon on the Mount, often read as a précis of Christianity, has nothing in it about Jesus' "saving" passion, death, and resurrection, not even in the quintessential Christian prayer, the Our Father. When Jesus predicts in his coming death—in passages (e.g., Mt. 16.21) that read like after-the-fact interpolations—he doesn't explain *why* he has to die. And then he ruins everything by wrongly predicting that, "Verily ... there be some standing here, which shall not taste of death, till they see the Son of man coming in his kingdom" (Mt. 16.28). (N.b., whatever else the elusive messianic title "son of man" may imply or allude to, it plainly designates its bearer to be a human being—the New Revised Standard Version translates it as "mortal"—and here Jesus was human enough to be flat wrong.)

Jesus' boldest assertion was that he could and did forgive sin. When he forgives *and* cures the paralytic (Mt. 9.1-8; Mk. 2.1-12; Lk. 5.17-26), some of the religious experts in the audience think (to themselves) that he's blaspheming. But Jesus reads their minds and defiantly does what only God can do. Then at the Last Supper he takes a quantum leap and declares, "This is my blood of the new testament, which is shed for many for the remission of sins" (Mt. 26.28). Whatever Jesus may have actually said, Christians followed John the Baptist's lead in thinking of him as the antitype of the Paschal lamb, "which taketh away the sins of the world" (Jn. 1.29) and as Abraham's sacrificial ram (even while claiming for himself, or having the Evangelists claim for him, the divine role of the Good Shepherd, borrowed from Ezekiel 34).

And so the stage is set for Paul's lunatic doctrine of salvation, as expounded in the Letter to the Romans and elsewhere. But before going into that, one has to wonder how this magical pardon works, the one that Jesus gave first to isolated individuals and next to the entire human race or at least to the believers who accepted him. For starters, what concrete difference does such forgiveness make? In the case of the paralytic and other sufferers cured by Jesus, the physical change was immediate, drastic, and long-lasting. But forgiveness doesn't alter the past nor undo any of the old damage (for example, to the human victims of mistreatment). And what exactly does God have to do with it—other than adding up an extra dimension of guilt, of course? Is it like committing a crime in a national monument, thereby making it, in addition to everything else, a federal offense? Both curing a disease and forgiving a sin are as easy for Jesus as saying the magic word, but one has to question the value of such presumed "divine" erasure, and hence the very meaning, of sin.

Consider the eruption of guilt in Psalm 51, attributed to David, after being chided by the prophet Nathan for having sex with (i.e., raping) Bathsheba and sending her husband Uriah to his death: "Against thee only have I sinned, and done this evil in thy sight; ... Behold, I was shaped in iniquity: and in sin did my mother conceive me ...Purge me with hyssop, and I shall be clean: wash me, and I shall be whiter than snow ... Hide thy face from my sins, and blot out all my iniquities" (vv. 4-5, 7, 9). As far as we can tell, God complies with "David's" grief-stricken request to "fill him with joy and gladness," and so the guilt-phase, though not the punishment phase, is over. (The psalm doesn't mention the unnamed baby born from the adulterous act and soon killed by God [2 Sam. 12.18], presumably to teach David a lesson.) How fortunate for David to be forgiven by God, since Uriah's lips are forever sealed; and Bathsheba, if she kept her wits about her, never brought up the subject again.

But really, this is beyond the pale, an absurd legal fiction just waiting to be carried to a still higher level of absurdity by Christian theologians. Jews dealt with sin-guilt by repentance, prayer, fasting, and occasional orgies of verbal self-flagellation, notably on Yom Kippur (cf. the *vidui*, or confession: "We have incurred guilt, we have betrayed, stolen, slandered, caused perversion and wickedness. We have deliberately sinned, extorted, made false accusations and given false counsel. We have been deceptive, scornful, rebellious, provocative, headstrong, perverse, wanton, persecutors, obstinate, wicked, corrupt, abominable, and deviant.") As James Thurber might say, "I can't tell from your communication whether you wish advice or are just boasting." "Sinfulness" is sexy.

Paul took the Jewish notion of sin and extrapolated it to infinity. Jewish sacred history had been all about astonishing fertility and rescue from danger, culminating in the gift of the Law. Paul was a celibate with no interest in children, who started out from the despairing assumption that the Law didn't work, and who therefore looked to an astonishing rescue from his misery, which he conflated with the human condition. Moses had said the law was doable (Deut. 30.11-14), not "hidden," nor remote, "very nigh unto thee, in thy mouth, and in thy heart, that thou mayest do it." No way, shouted Paul. "For what I would, that I do not, but what I hate, that do I" (Rom. 7.15). Sin, he laments, has taken over within him, Putting it still more ominously, "Sin revived, and I died" (v. 7). The good news, of course, is that, along with the disease, Paul had also discovered the cure: "Therefore being justified by faith, we have peace with God through our Lord Jesus Christ" (Rom. 5.1).

The only catch was, it took a heavy dosage of magical thinking to make this scheme work. First, a return to corporate guilt: "As in Adam all die, even so in Christ shall all be made alive" (1 Cor. 15.22). Thus we get what's probably the most far-fetched, influential, and insane midrash of all time: By disobeying God, Adam (whom Genesis sees not as an individual person, but a generic human being) contracts an ontological debt that only Jesus can pay off by taking the sacrifice of Isaac all the way to the end. (In *The Death and Resurrection of the Beloved Son* [1995], Prof. Jon Levinson reminds us that some rabbis believed Isaac *had* been killed and burnt to ashes, but had risen again. The Genesis text, after all, makes no mention of Isaac in the final verse of the story: "So Abraham returned unto his young men, and they arose and went together to Beer-sheba, and Abraham dwelt at Beer-sheba" [22.19]). Thus, the death of Jesus was like the death of Isaac multiplied by the biggest number you can think of. If Christianity (Paul) neither would nor could compete with Moses, it would seek to surpass Abraham.

Thus Paul gives us the myth of original sin or, as the Germans call it, "hereditary sin" (*Erbsünde*), with Adam and Jesus as the twin poles of history. (Never mind that there was no single progenitor of the human race.) Like Paul, we can't reach moral goodness on our own, so we hitch our helpless little cars to Jesus' mighty locomotive; and off we go. As Anselm of Canterbury (d. 1109) explained it in *Why God (Became) Man*, an offense against an infinite God is an infinite offense committed by a finite creature and hence requires an infinitely great sin-offering to give "satisfaction" to an all-demanding God. Only Jesus fills the bill, and so we're saved. Judaism was all about obeying the Law; Christianity was all about the relief you felt at being forgiven for your failure to obey it. Given the intensely psychological nature of their faith, it's no surprise that, as time went on, Christians would invent a myriad of personal mental apps: devotions, cultic practices, and fissiparous heresies.

Meantime, there wasn't much hard physical evidence for this earth-shaking turn of events (as Nietzsche suggested in *Thus Spoke Zarathustra*, "The Priests," Jesus' disciples don't *look* all that redeemed), so Christians had to focus on the world to come, especially when the Messiah's Parousia kept getting put off. And Paul's uplifting notion of celestial life didn't make it any less vague. In 1 Cor. 15.35-58 he's hard pressed to answer the skeptic who wants to know, "How are the dead raised up? And with what body do they come?" The best he can devise is the abstract formula that, "It (a corpse) is sown in corruption, it is raised in incorruption. It is sown in dishonor, it is raised in glory: it is sown in weakness, it is raised in power: it is sown a natural body, it is raised a spiritual body." Jesus had offered that metaphor of a seed falling into the ground, "dying," and being transformed into new life (Jn. 12.24); but sprouting seeds *don't* die; and there few things more unlike a seed than a cadaver.

Feeble and blurry as it was, the promise of resurrection solved the problem of the Deuteronomic Principle: Honesty demanded the admission that the good often go unrewarded and the wicked often go unpunished—"under the sun" at any rate. But a great Second-and-Final Act could set all that straight. All the trillions of history's loose ends could be neatly straightened out and tied up. The bloody apocalyptic hysteria of Revelation may have gone too far; but decades, if not centuries, of suffering *will* breed passionate impatience. And visions of a heavenly choir singing thunderous Amens provided both consolation for heartsick hopers and seekers, and the joy of seeing, or imagining one saw, what practically everyone had been looking for: a shape to history, the "closure" that American psychobabblers can never praise enough.

Once the golden glow of the Hallelujah Chorus has faded, however, a host of brain-splitting issues remain: Since humans are forever disagreeing about right and wrong—and humans are the only source of information about God's view of morality—how can we know for sure what (and how serious) a sin is? What is the proportionality between human misbehavior and "time served" (in whichever world)? How could there be eternal duration in heaven or hell (both equally preposterous), since nothing is ever the same from moment to moment, and nothing can be truthfully said to last? Why is the Afterlife populated exclusively by humans (and some angels, with no animals at all)? Even if the problem of evil is finally "taken care of" when the last trumpet blows, why does God let it happen in the first place? (What a stupid waste!) What would the meaning of repentance be in a world *without* God? What's the empirical difference between a forgiven and an unforgiven sin? (How about imagining two contrasting scenarios in which a) the Japanese authorities and soldiers responsible for the Rape of Nanjing decide that they're heartily sorry for the whole thing, and b) they don't so decide? How much is that "sorry" worth? And finally, why should anyone believe a word of such starry-eyed rhapsodizing? Why not go for the houris and some Allah-supplied Viagra? (The ladies will have to look out for themselves.)

So, let's see, how far have we come from our First Chapter of salvation history, the story of Abraham? Assuming for the sake of argument that Jesus is the "Word of God," then we've made a lot of progress since the hasty, elusive theophanies of Genesis have been replaced by a lengthy, up-close-and-personal presentation by God's own "Son" (though that term defies coherent explanation). Granted, much of what he says sounds like a vivid reworking of the Torah, along with hints (expanded by Paul) about "redemption," and some picturesque, but hardly credible apocalyptic-eschatological scenarios. But the stories have drama and power, unlike Muhammad's ramblings. If what they add up to is the claim that God is very much like Jesus, then we do know more about Him than we did from Abraham's adventures. Still, all the metaphysical puzzles Jesus is supposed to solve remain baffling. E.g., what exactly is "the Holy Spirit"? And, though Jesus is millennia closer to us in time than Abraham (if *he* ever lived), the miracles that fly every which way through the Gospels (and Acts) carry the figure of Jesus far out of historical sight.

The Son's-Sacrifice part of Christianity is gripping but inconclusive, especially if the reader has no interest in having God arrange for someone die "for" her or him. To Paul's argument that Jesus is "a propitiation through faith in his blood" (Rom. 3.25), Nietzsche replies: "Blood is the worst witness to the truth; blood poisons the truest teaching and turns it into madness and heartfelt hatred" (*Thus Spoke Zarathustra*, II, iv). For all their claims that Jesus' death was "good," New Testament writers persist in blaming "the Jews" (both leaders and the masses) for the execution of Jesus, which was a Roman operation from start to finish. ("His blood be on us and on our children," Mt. 27.25, takes us back to all those Old Testament scenes [Josh. 24.16, etc], where "the people" cry out as one, and thereby go on record against themselves.) As with the aborted sacrifice of Isaac, the sacrifice of Jesus (which Muhammad said never happened, 4:157), the ultimate proof of faith by one chosen individual leads to promises of sensational future bliss. And so on.

Thus, the central Old Testament figure for Christianity isn't Moses, the Taskmaster, but Abraham the Believer. Since Abraham was found to be righteous long before—and sans any help from—Moses, there was no dodging the fateful conclusion that," a man is justified by faith without the works of the law" (Rom. 3.28). No one but crazy Paul would have gone still further and dreamt up the allegorical misreading proffered in Galatians 4.21-26, 28-31, which knocks Genesis on its ear:

> Tell me, ye that desire to be under the law, do ye not hear the law? For it is written that Abraham had two sons, the one by a

bondmaid, the other by a freewoman. But he who was of the bondwoman was born after the flesh: but he of the freewoman was by promise. Which things are an allegory: for these are the two covenants: the one from mount Sinai which gendereth to bondage, which is Agar. For this Agar is mount Sinai in Arabia, and answereth to Jerusalem which now is, and is in bondage with her children. But Jerusalem which is above is free, which is the mother of us all. … Now we, brethren, as Isaac was, are the children of promise. But as then he that was born after the flesh persecuted him that was born after the spirit, even so it is now. Nevertheless what saith the scripture? "Cast out the bondwoman and her son: for the son of the bondwoman shall not be heir with the son of the freewoman." So then, brethren, we are not children of the bondwoman, but of the free.

It's a beautiful example of the Humpty-Dumpty semantics favored by the Abrahamists, who are liable to say *anything*, and insist their sacred texts mean whatever they want them to mean. Egyptian Hagar is the synagogue (Mount Sinai, and hence the Jews), Sarah is the church; so Jews are Gentiles (as the Mormons like to say). A short walk down this twisting road will take you to Dante's declaration that hell was built by "Primal Love."

Now that Paul and other Christians have figured out how history works—everything from the resurrection of Jesus onward is just a more or less anxious waiting period for Judgment—the focus shifts to the rules Christians have to follow while waiting. And at first blush it seems that the Christian code is very different from the Torah; for the game has radically changed. As Paul says," Abraham our father" (Rom. 4.1) lived long before the Law was given to Moses; therefore couldn't have been saved by "works." (Generations of Calvinist preachers have spoken of "works righteousness" with lip-curling contempt.) God, in fact, saved Abraham even before he was circumcised, because of Abraham's "faith" (trust) in him. And so he does with us, "for all have sinned, and come short of the glory of God, being justified freely by his grace through the redemption that is in Jesus Christ: whom God hath set forth to be a propitiation ..." (Rom. 3.23-25). A "propitiation"—once again we're busy softening up The Angry Old Man.

The Law manifestly couldn't save you; all it did was point out your failures and worsen your guilt. In one of those paradoxical utterances that have not endeared him to Jews, Paul insists that, "Christ hath redeemed us from the curse of the law" (Gal. 3.13). But at the same time Paul was aware that declaring the Law cancelled might sound like swinging the door open to antinomian license. If God is the Ultimate Rich Uncle, don't all Christians have an unlimited line of credit? "What shall we say then? Shall we continue in sin, that grace may abound? God forbid" (Rom. 6.1-2). But the fact that antinomianism ("Sin bravely," as Luther said) kept raising its rascally head in the Church, from the Gnostics to the Albigensians to the Ranters and beyond (not to mention the untold Catholic hordes who've been happy to treat confession as a get-out-of-jail-free card) shows that the danger was a real one.

Augustine's celebrated *dilige, et quod vis fac* (Tractatus VII, 8) has a wonderful ring to it; but, realistically, how many people can be trusted to just love (God) and then do what they want? In fact, Christians took over most key sections of the Jewish moral code, starting with the Decalogue. They added to the mix Jesus' extremist demands (see below), mostly downgraded to mere suggestions for devout overachievers; the "natural law," which was amazingly apt to coincide with church law; and eventually the long, detailed Code of Canon Law. After Jesus' fierce harangues against the "scribes" (legal experts), the Catholic Church went out and got its own brand of scribes, who could explain such niceties as why using the rhythm method to avoid pregnancy was all well and good, but using condoms or the pill was a mortal sin.

And so, the Christian churches didn't simply abandon the Torah. They did greatly simplify things for the growing masses of gentile converts by abolishing circumcision, ending dietary rules, dropping the entire Jewish liturgy—no more tallit, tefillin, tzitzit, black fasts on Yom Kippur and the Ninth of Av, no more obsessive removal of *hametz* for Passover, etc. And no more need to study the Law. One could, like Paul, be a fool for Christ (2 Cor. 11.21) or even a full time crazy, a "holy fool," (*yurodivy*, in the Russian style). The three theological (i.e., most sublime, unattainable by mere human effort) virtues were faith, hope, and charity, not brains, wit, and perspicacity.

Countless other *mitzvot* go by the board, but some major traditions are maintained, including slavery, misogyny, and homophobia. Since Jesus and Paul placed so much emphasis on universal brotherhood and sisterhood, one might have expected them or later Christian leaders to call for the freeing of slaves; but until modern times nobody did. Besides, didn't Noah's curse on Ham/Canaan (Gen. 9.25, 27) constitute divine authorization of the African slave trade? Jesus (whose mission was bankrolled by the rich women mentioned in Luke 8.2) displayed an open and friendly attitude toward women, and women were active in the first few generations of the "primitive church." But, with increasing institutionalization, the old rabbinical attitudes took over: Paul had already called for women to keep silent in church (1 Cor. 14.24); and the writer pretending to be Paul some years later in 1 Timothy sealed the deal with pronouncements like "Let the woman learn in silence with all subjection. But I suffer not a woman to teach, nor to usurp authority over the man, but to be in silence. For Adam was first formed, then Eve. And Adam was not deceived, but the woman being deceived was in the transgression. Notwithstanding she shall be saved in child-bearing, if they continue in faith and charity and holiness with sobriety (2.11-15).

The same epistle complains, fittingly enough, about younger widows: as the only women both not under male control and still full of unused energy, they were bound to cause all sorts of headaches for stressed-out ecclesiastical CEOs. And Paul expanded the

Old Testament hatred of gays by including lesbians for the first time in the category of sinner "against nature" (Rom. 1.26). To no one's surprise, Muhammad would later agree.

But Christian patriarchy had one new wrinkle: the very un-Jewish cult of celibacy. While Jesus' marital status is unclear, Paul stoutly championed his unmarried condition for, among other reasons, the imminence of world's end. On the other hand, in seeing sex as a bothersome distraction ("It is good for a man not to touch a woman," 1 Cor. 7.1), Paul wasn't that far from the rabbis. In the Pirke Avot, Yose ben Yochanan of Jerusalem says, "The Sages said: The man who spends too much time in idle talk with women will bring trouble upon himself; he neglects to study the Torah and will ultimately inherit Gehinnom," I,5. And Hillel adds, "The more flesh, the more rottenness ... The more women there are, the more superstition there will be; the more maid-servants, the more lustfulness "(II, 8,). Best get that lust out of your system by early marriage, then off to the Bet Midrash.

But the unbiblical Catholic refusal to allow a married clergy, currently under scrutiny because of the metastasizing scandal of priestly pedophilia, made it much easier to invent and hold on to the cockeyed prohibition against "artificial" contraception. Though widely ignored, that ban, along with its stands demonizing abortion, divorce, masturbation, etc., inclines one to say that everything the Catholic Church has ever said about sex was wrong. Not that most other Christian churches had a strikingly better record.

No doubt this was more or less inevitable. After all, the foundational monotheistic story of Abraham casts the inferiority of women in stone. Their sterility was a major obstacle to male and tribal hopes, overcome only by God's transcendent power. Sarah's attractiveness posed a life-threatening danger for her husband, and her jealousy and nastiness made his life miserable. Abraham acquired wives or concubines as needed, and the ladies were locked up in the women's quarters. (That was fine with Christian patriarchs and

Muhammad.) Apart from their indispensable breeding capacity, women were irrelevant to the God-man dialogue. Of course, God's name, way of speaking, and metaphors were all masculine. The Christian cult of Mary brought back the hitherto repressed goddess-figure; but she was always depicted as humble, submissive, and non-threatening. It was only logical that Catholic nuns should be treated as third-class citizens. So much for Paul's hopeful remark that, "There is neither bond nor free, there is neither male nor female; for ye are all one in Christ Jesus" (Gal. 3.28).

Indeed, one has to ask what positive contribution have Christian theologians made to ethics with their interminable regulating and anathematizing? Jesus' most radical moral demands (love your enemies, give away your fortune to the poor, turn the other cheek, let yourself be robbed, go the extra mile—though that last one has been hijacked and trivialized by State Farm and others) have never found many takers among his nominal followers. Then again, his order not to resist evil (Mt. 5.39), sounds like a bad idea and best ignored altogether. Jesus apparent rejection of divorce has caused all sorts of problems; but Christians have ignored this hard line, while the proudly inflexible Roman Catholics have found the handy tool of annulment to get around it.

On political and social issues, most Christians have been content to accept Paul's dictum that, "The powers that be are ordained of God. Whosoever therefore resisteth the power, resisteth the ordinance of God; and they that resist shall receive to themselves damnation" (Rom. 13.1-2) and have adjusted comfortably to the dictators, tyrants, and autocrats heaven has blessed them with. Germany's Lutheran clergy gave a particularly striking demonstration of this during the Third Reich; and Catholics loyally supported not just Hitler, but Mussolini, Franco, Salazar, Pétain, et al. Much of the New Testament has a politically quietist flavor, as seen in The Pastoral Epistles, the Letters of Peter, etc. After all, people who take themselves to be, as the author of 1 Peter 2.11 says, "strangers and pilgrims" (cf. Heb. 11.13, "strangers and pilgrims on the earth") have little reason to get mixed up with or bothered by the passing illusions of worldly business. Muhammad often dwells on this notion in the Qur'an: "The life of this world is but a sport and a diversion. It is the life to come that is the true life: if they but knew it" (29:64). The great monotheists were forever reminding their followers to pray, fast, sacrifice, and suffer—but not to vote, organize, or rock the boat. (They would, however, be allowed to fight and kill for their religion.)

With their glance (theoretically, at least, and often actually) fixed on the afterlife, their exaltation of sexual purity (as in the monastic movement and consecrated sisterhood), Christian moralists did their best to devalue sex and the flesh in general. Like their Jewish forebears, they mostly ignored animals and the environment, since such things had no moral standing, except insofar as they were human property. The New Jerusalem in Revelation (chapters 21-22) was an entirely mineral affair, with only one plant, the tree of life, and a fishless, frogless "pure river of water of life" (22.1) flowing through the City. Monotheism, in general, has no idea what to do with animals, except exploit and eat them.

The key to Christian life was faith-and-obedience, as Abraham had believed and obeyed God, and Isaac had believed and obeyed Abraham. Yes, the New Covenant, like the Old one, had opened all sorts of splendid vistas: a whole new way of being, even as Abram's name had been changed and he had been granted a biologically impossible son. And there were promises of future happiness (hosts of Israelites like the sands of the sea in the Land of Canaan=the chorus of the redeemed in Paradise). But the tenor of everyday existence was doing what you were told, following like sheep. As Christopher Hitchens notes in *Hitch -22*, "Everything about Christianity is contained in the pathetic image of 'the flock.' Whence the pastors, folds, crosiers, and endless talk about the Good Shepherd.

Trusting obedience had been Abraham's great virtue (though Abraham also argued with God about Sodom, a prophetic trait that soon went out of style), and it was Isaac-Jesus' virtue too, as illustrated by the "Agony in the Garden": "And he went a little farther, and fell on his face, and prayed, saying, 'O my Father, if it be possible, let this cup pass from me: nevertheless not as I will, but as thou wilt '"[i.e., let me be murdered] (Mt. 26.39). Obedience would be the watchword of Ignatius Loyola, who in a pair of famous similes bid his followers display the selfless passivity of a corpse or a staff in an old man's hand (Constitutions, Part VI, Chapter 1).

On this point Ignatius was only echoing a much older tradition, enshrined, for example, in the Rule of St. Benedict, which calls for far more than mere compliance: "But this very obedience will be acceptable to God and pleasing to men only if what is commanded is done without hesitation, delay, lukewarmness, grumbling or objection. ... For if the disciple obeys with an ill will and murmurs, not necessarily with his lips but simply in his heart, then even though he fulfill the command, nevertheless his work will not be acceptable to God, who sees that his heart is murmuring. And, far from gaining a reward for such work as this, he will incur the punishment due to murmurers, unless he makes amends and gives satisfaction" (Chapter V). And, as we'll see, Muslims too, whose very name denotes submission and connotes slavish prostration in the dust, enthusiastically carry on this Abrahamic theme of obedience. When God (through his representative) gives the orders, you can't go wrong. But at least Abraham was never forbidden to indulge in a few internal "murmurs" (or so we like to imagine him doing).

What probably lies at the bottom of it all this is infantile regression. Mightn't all monotheistic religion be summed up as follows: Man "finds" Father; man worships Father; man does what he thinks (tells himself) Father wants? The order to sacrifice the son establishes who's *really* the boss, the one with the life-and-death *patria potestas* ("Soy tu padre," as Mexicans often say). One surrenders one's independence, one gains lifetime security: a baby forever. On the other hand, the male religious leaders, as the spokesmen for, and official authorities on, the Almighty's wishes, also drape themselves in borrowed versions of God's power and importance. Judaism and Islam often boast of not having a clergy (in the Catholic sense of essential intermediaries between God and humanity); but in all fields, including religion, modern people distinguish sharply between experts and amateurs; and the experts call the shots. Consider Iran's Guardian Council.

The rabbis, priests, ministers, mullahs, etc. are all, to a greater or lesser extent, father figures; and many of them are actually called "Father." Among Orthodox Jews, Eastern Orthodox Christians, Muslims, and conservative clergy as a whole they are generally characterized by bushy beards, long robes, and solemn faces: domineering, often overweight, papas and patriarchs, a whole batch of Abrahams. Now more than ever we need to get rid of them.

Perhaps the simplest way to encourage people to do this might be the thought-experiment of trying to retell the Aqedah, and the Christian elaborations on it, with a feminine cast. Imagine Sarah being visited by YHWH and asked to sacrifice her daughter (her only child). Of course, she would have vehemently refused—just another instance of the way women often let personal, emotional considerations impinge on Lawrence-Kohlberg-type moral imperatives .Better yet, imagine Yahweh himself as female. Would she have wasted a nano-second mulling over such a cruel, pointless test of a mother's love?

And would the Christian doctrine of Redemption, Propitiation, Substituionary Atonement, etc. work with a Mother-Daughter combination? Would a Goddess contemplate the sacrifice of her daughter to patch up matters with the misbehaving human race? Would She have flown the cockamamie Christian scheme of redemption-through-blood past an incredulous Mary (whose daughters the Evangelists don't bother to name)?

Rhetorical questions, one and all. The story of Abraham is one male fantasy upon another (e.g., God the King of the Gay-bashers)—not that sensible men wouldn't reject it too, as many have. Feminize the story, and it collapses of its own weight. Its components are testosterone-saturated: the Vengeful Judge, the Registrar of Wrongs (*Judex ergo cum sedebit/ Quidquid latet apparebit/ Nil inultum remanebit*), the Omnipotent Father, Christ Pantocrator (take *that*, slimy Arians!), the King of Glory, "and behold, a white horse: and he that sat on him had a bow, and a crown was given unto him, and he went forth conquering and to conquer" (Rev. 6.2) And why not throw in a *Hagios Ischyros* and a *Rex tremendae majestatis* while we're at it?

The usual liberal Christian response to such instances of hairy-chested holiness is to cough discreetly and dismiss them as obsolete metaphors. Well, they *are* metaphors—the only possible way to speak about a non-physical, non-spatio-temporal deity—but they're hardly obsolete. They illustrate the way that ever since Abraham monotheists habitually think about and describe the object of their awe. To date they have yet to produce any serious alternatives. How could they, given the overwhelming masculine bias of their texts and traditions? As we've seen, Abrahamite theology comes down to the visions of male narcissists—the prophets and their pals—staring into their Pool of Faith and seeing an idealized image of themselves. Christian prophets (all the New Testament authors and the swarming commentariat they begot) have to be credited with assembling the most creative, colorful, and crazy of all the Abrahamic myths. Their success is shown by the ubiquitous crosses on churches and in cemeteries all over the planet, on the walls of Catholic schools, hospitals, and bedrooms, as well as in its lesser role as a talisman etched in tattoos or hung on ears, necks, and rearview mirrors in cars, and as a ritual gesture to improve a batter's chances at the plate. If your game, athletic, religious, or otherwise, is magical thinking, why not go all the way?

Chapter Three

Abraham, the First Muslim

When his Lord put Abraham to the proof by enjoining on him certain commandments and Abraham fulfilled them, He said, "I have appointed you a leader of mankind."
"And what of my descendants?" asked Abraham.
"My covenant," said He, "does not apply to the evil-doers."
We made the House [=the Ka'aba] a resort and a sanctuary for mankind, saying: "Make the place where Abraham stood a house of worship." We enjoined Abraham and Ishmael to cleanse Our House for those who walk round it, who meditate in it, and who kneel and prostrate themselves.
"Lord," said Abraham, "make this a secure land and bestow plenty upon its people, those of them that believe in God and the Last Day."
"As for those who do not," He answered, "I shall let them live awhile, and then shall drag them to the scourge of the Fire: an evil fate."
Abraham and Ishmael built the House and dedicated it, saying: "Accept this from us, Lord. You are the One that hears all and knows all. Lord, make us submissive to You; make of our descendants a community that will submit to You. ... Lord, send forth to them an apostle of their own who shall declare to them Your revelations, and instruct them in the Book and in wisdom, and shall purify them of sin. You are the Mighty, the Wise One."

Who but a foolish man would renounce the faith of Abraham?

—Qur'an 2:123-130, tr. N. J. Dawood

You call *that* a story? The first thing that strikes an unbelieving, non-Arabic reader of the Qur'an is Muhammad's deplorable lack of narrative talent. In this passage, for instance, the first verses in the Qur'an to mention Abraham, we get little more than stodgy bits of dialogue. The dramatic, nearly heart-breaking events of the Binding are passed over as "certain commandments" enjoined by Allah. Abraham and Ishmael, not Isaac, are hauled hundreds of miles down to Mecca, where Ibrahim prays on behalf of the Arabs and does some promotional work for Muhammad and the Muslims. (Through a genealogy as fishy as anything in Matthew's and Luke's, Muslims claim Abraham as Muhammad's ancestor, through Ishmael and the father of the northern Arabs, Adnan.) Abraham and Ishmael build the Ka'aba, and at some point (chronology was not one of Muhammad's skills either) clean it up, presumably removing the pagan accouterments that it had acquired by Muhammad's own day.

Of course, any praise lavished on Abraham might conceivably be viewed as bolstering the Jews; so Muhammad wastes no time in getting that perverse notion out of the way. Early on in the Qur'an (2:140, 3:67) we are sternly advised that Abraham was neither a Jew nor a Christian. He may be, Muhammad admits, a divinely appointed "leader of mankind," but his (grr) "descendants" are immediately dismissed as "evildoers," though that might not apply to every single one of them. As so often in the Qur'an, Allah loves to spout threats about the hellish torture awaiting the infidels. All those who happen not to believe in God and the Last Day will be dragged away to the "scourge of Fire." The first unwelcome sensation Hell inflicts is a jolt of ghastly surprise.

Abraham and Ishmael, who are not described in any way whatsoever, pray on and on, not forgetting to prophesy the coming of Muhammad himself: "an apostle of their own, who shall declare to them Your revelations, and instruct them in the Book and in wisdom, and shall purify them of sin." This method of reading back into the Scriptures the presence of things that the original writers never dreamed of was perfected by the authors of the New Testament, above all Matthew; and then clumsily imitated by Muhammad, who, even if he wasn't illiterate, had only a muddled notion of Jewish traditions. Muhammad's "tales" are surely just as fictional as the great bulk of the Bible's, just not very good fiction.

Worse yet, Muslims are taught to believe that the Qur'an is the "flawless" (39:28) eternal word of God himself, which outlaws any kind of meaningful textual criticism and would put any Muslim who said anything like what I've said and will say about the Qur'an in serious physical danger. But scripture-worship (whatever The Book says goes) is a legacy to Islam from Judaism and Christianity. And, thanks to the limited approval bestowed by Muhammad on the People of the Book, he was able to lay claim to his own skewed version of sacred history. Like the Mormons, both Christians and Muslims had no intention of starting from scratch. They were in a hurry, and old-fashioned religious traditions take generations to create, so they had to beg, borrow, and steal on a grand scale. Unfortunately, Muhammad (a sincere visionary dreamer) and Smith (a boring faker) were only individual men; and thus their pious maundering results in deadly monotony, unlike the more varied New Testament and the splendidly polyphonic Hebrew Bible.

Does it matter that Muhammad lacked the precious asset of his own large scriptural library, with varying sources and multiple authors? That he was thrown back on his volatile prophetic temperament, passionate, sometimes furious, and resentful? From a literary point of view, it certainly does. It's one thing when Mark has Jesus speak of hell as a place, "where their worm dieth not and the fire is not quenched (9.44); but Allah makes a much worse impression when he personally promises, "*I shall drag them* to the scourge of the Fire." Doesn't he have anything better to do, like oversee a few nebulae, than play the role of a micro-managing Nazi camp commandant?

On the other hand, does Muhammad's *Unbeholfenheit* in telling the crucial story of the first believer really matter, given that the general drift is clear? For example, in the reworked scene with the heavenly messengers at the oaks of Mamre, Muhammad may have been offended by the notion of angels actually eating human food, as they do in Gen. 18.8, so he merely has Abraham asking, "Will you not eat?" (51.27). In a non-sequitur they reply, "Have no fear," and tell him "he [is] to have a son endowed with knowledge." At that point Sarah comes out "crying and beating her face. "Surely I am a barren old woman." "Such is the will of your Lord," the angels impassively declare. "He is the Wise One, the All-knowing"—though how any human, massively ignorant like all his conspecifics, could know that any other person was "all-knowing" is hard to figure. Then they proceed to the momentous task of nuking Sodom and Gomorrah.

When Muhammad gets around to the Aqedah, it's an anti-climax, almost a throwaway. "We gave him news of a gentle son [no name or mother given]. And when he reached the age when he could work with him, his father said to him: 'My son, I dreamt that I was sacrificing you. Tell me what you think.' [Here imagine your own unprintable response.] He replied: 'Father, do as you are bidden. God willing, you shall find me steadfast.' And when they had both submitted to God, and Abraham had laid down his son prostrate upon his face, We called out to him, saying: "Abraham, you have fulfilled your vision." [A feeble substitute for "Lay not thy hand upon the lad"] Allah goes on: "Thus do we reward the righteous. That was indeed a bitter test. We ransomed his son with a noble sacrifice" (37:101-107). ["We" ransomed? You mean, "we" graciously accepted one male victim in place of another. Aren't "we" generous! And what exactly makes the sacrifice "noble"?]

It's not just a problem with Abraham and Isaac-Ishmael. Muhammad does no better with other major biblical figures like Joseph, Moses, or Jesus. The tale of Joseph in Genesis is one of the Bible's masterpieces, packed with tension, quarrels, and surprises. In Muhammad's adaptation it becomes flat, preachy, and colorless. But there's no need for Muslims to worry about that since the Prophet's stories already had been told and written down, if anyone wanted to read them. Nor does he provide much of an autobiography, in the manner of Jeremiah or Paul. On the other hand, Islam soon developed its own sacred history in the triumphant career of the Prophet's message through Arabia and, after his death, the world, in striking contrast to the Jews, who never got to dominate anything, and the Christians, who had to wait for centuries before arriving in the seats of power.

But there was a downside to this. The sacred history of Islam's almost-always-victorious surge, as retold in the Qur'an, the hadiths, and early Muslim historians, wasn't carefully edited with an eye to the sensibilities of later ages; and so episodes emerged that look embarrassing when viewed through the microscope of secular objectivity, rather than the telescope of what Gibbon might have called supine enthusiasm. The vicissitudes of life in Muhammad's harem, for example, his acquisition of his adopted son Zayd's delectable wife Zaynab, or the squabbles over his dalliance with his Coptic concubine Mariya, or the "marriage" with his luscious Jewish captive Saffiya, after putting her husband to death for hiding booty, make it hard for westerners to share the breathless Muslim veneration for the Messenger of God. Muhammad's career as a warrior, in the battles of Badr, Uhud, and the Trench likewise make him sound like just another warlord, a level that he may even be said to slip beneath in his mass murder (600-900 men) and despoliation of the Banu Qurayza Jews. (For details on these matters, see

Maxime Rodinson, *Muhammad,* tr. Anne Carter, New Press, 1990). "Generalissimo" and "flawless holy man" don't fit comfortably into the same job description.

Muslim chroniclers saw no difficulty in describing Muhammad's raids and pillaging, any more than in their reporting of how he had satirical poets Asma bint Marwn and Abu Afak assassinated for mocking him. (We may recall the frankness of 2 Samuel in recounting David's thuggish behavior.) Assuming there was a divine purpose in all the blood spilled by Muhammad, what does it tell us about Islamic *Heilsgeschichte* that three of the first four caliphs, Omar, Uthman, and Ali were murdered, like Ali's three sons, Husayn, Abbas, and Hasan? That Sunnis and Shias have been killing one another for over thirteen hundred years (much like Catholics and Protestants, western Christians and eastern Orthodox)? Do we know whose side Allah is on?

But where Muslims see holy warriors, westerners see plain warriors, a profession we've learned to distrust, if not despise, especially after the 20th century. We can share the disgust or rage felt by Muslims for Crusaders and colonialists; but we wonder why they have no problems with Arab imperialism in Persia, India, North Africa, or Spain. And even though 4:29 says right out, "Do not kill yourselves," somehow the mullahs and imams pass over in silence the ravages of Islamist suicide bombers that are a front-page news item almost every day of the week. Most of us have lost patience with the *Dominus Deus Sabaoth.*

Besides, those Islamic conquests are many centuries old; and the Islamic world today is a political, juridical, economic, intellectual, scientific, and cultural disaster area. Only maniacs still dream of the Caliphate (or the appearance of the Twelfth Imam). What Muslims most need now is education, contraception, women's rights, health care, and social justice, not more faith. And on these subjects Islam doesn't have much useful to say or to offer. The torrents of abuse that Muhammad heaps on the heads of sinners mostly refer to unbelief and hatred of Allah's awesome Messenger, not to crimes against humanity. And how much would a possibly illiterate 7th century Arabian merchant know about humanity anyway?

Secularists can be grateful for the clarity with which the latter centuries of Islamic history (which would have to include numerous invasions of Europe, the Armenian and Sudanese genocides, the African slave trade, the widespread making and exploiting of eunuchs, etc.) show once again how the very notion of sacred history is a chimera. Of course, going back to dreams of an imaginary sacred time, as all the monotheistic religions do, is just as nonsensical as Homer's claim that warriors like Hector, Aeneas, and Diomedes could heave huge rocks that latter-day weaklings couldn't even lift. Such devolution, as seen for instance in the decreasing life expectancy of the biblical patriarchs, makes believers rhapsodize over an unreachable primeval past, which they hope to experience in some sort of apocalyptic, messianic, divine End of Time.

But extrapolating to the blessed there from the wretched here and now gets harder and harder. The faithful can happily pretend that God used to intervene in human lives with gratifying frequency; but not now. What has Allah done for Muslims lately? Smooth transitions to democracy? Nobel Prizes? World Cups? Is there anything wrong with Muslim cultures that a tool kit of secular remedies couldn't help? Surely it's not a coincidence that western progress in democracy, rational social arrangements, medicine and science in general, took place during an age when religion was losing its grip on people's minds, and tolerance, born of agnosticism and religious indifference, opened the door to all sorts of advances. And, as with archaic Jewish and Christian morality, does any reflective person really think that Sharia has anything to teach us today that we don't already know? If so, what? Bigoted Christian fear-mongers in states like Oklahoma and publicity hounds like Pastor Terry Jones enjoy conjuring up the phantasm of "Sharia law" spreading across America—about as likely as all the players in the NBA quitting basketball to become Buddhist monks. Despite the countless benighted Muslims pressing for its reintroduction, in the long run Sharia in the modern world is doomed. Among other things, God never made any laws.

The revelation of the divine Law to Moses came amid a sensational sound-and-light show, if you can believe Exodus 19.16, 18: "There were thunders and lightnings, and a thick cloud upon the mount, and the voice of the trumpet exceeding loud. So that all the people that was in the camp trembled …And mount Sinai was altogether on a smoke, because the LORD descended upon it in fire, and the smoke thereof ascended as the smoke of a furnace, and the whole mount quaked greatly." But special effects aren't reasons; and Allah's moral revelations to Muhammad, staged with much less fanfare, are just as useless as Moses', insofar as apodictic fee-fi-fo-fumming carries zero philosophical weight. Like Jews and Christians quoting the Bible, Muslims cite "proof texts" from the Qur'an or hadiths with door-slamming satisfaction, since God himself is taken to be their author. But that simply boils down to "Because I said so," which even five-year-olds learn to question.

And as with the Torah, Sharia turns out to be crammed full of bad ideas that crumble under serious criticism. Capital punishment, for starters, such as the hadith-mandated stoning for adultery (the Qur'an 24:2 calls for 100 lashes) or apostasy. All progressive countries on the planet have banned the death penalty, except for bastions of religious fanaticism like the USA or Iran. But the complete catalogue of barbaric laws is a long one. There's no need to blame all or most or even a lot of this on Muhammad, since he, like Moses, is a symbolic figure to whom all sors of traditions got attached, by way of heightening their importance. And unlike Moses, Muhammad isn't actually credited with much legislation, at least not in the Qur'an, which has nothing like the finicky lists of rules and regulations in Exodus, Leviticus and Deuteronomy.

But there's still plenty of sick sadism on display, for example in 5:34, "Those that make war against God and His apostle and spread disorders in the land shall be slain or crucified or have their hands and feet cut off on alternate sides ..." or 5:38: "As for the man or woman who is guilty of theft, cut off their hands to punish them for their crimes." One might naively suppose that this stupid law (still in effect, of course), coming from the Heavenly Horse's Mouth, might be enough to convince everyone of the non-divine provenance of the Qur'an; but one would be mistaken.

And the list goes on. Allah wants the Prophet to wage war on unbelievers and "hypocrites," i.e., wavering Muslims (9:73). Those who encourage Muslims to disbelieve are to be "seized and put to death wherever you find them" (4:89). Jihad—the military kind—is a religious duty. Revenge is a sacred obligation: "Retaliation is decreed for you in bloodshed: a free man for a free man, a slave for a slave, and a woman for a woman" (2:178, note the descending order). Polygyny (41:3) is cautiously endorsed (except for Muhammad himself, whose accumulation of extra females wins God's unstinting approval, as in 33:50). "Marriage" to prepubescent girls poses no problems (65:4). Women are to be veiled (33:59), are to inherit half what a male does (4:1); and when, if ever, they testify, it counts as half that of a man.

Men, Allah announces, have a status superior to women (2:228). Disobedient wives should be beaten (4:34). Fathers determine how long a child is to be nursed (2:233). Homosexuality is sternly condemned (4:16). Admitted lesbians are to be "confined to their houses till death overtakes them or till God finds another way for them" (4:15). Slavery is acceptable to Allah (30:28, etc.), as are slaughtering and eating animals (5:1) especially camels (22:36). Jews are roundly and repeatedly cursed (5:64, 5:82) because "Most of them are evil-doers" (3:111). Wine, along with games of chance, is forbidden as an "abomination designed by Satan (5:90). After urination, defecation, or ejaculation, men should wash their face and hands with water or, if none is available, sand (5:6). Menstruation is an illness, and menstruating women are "unclean" (2:222). Believers should never make friends with Jews and Christians, who are all in cahoots with one another (5:51). Anyone who doubts Muhammad's victories in this world and the next is advised to hang himself (22:15). And so forth.

So, after almost three millennia of God-struck stenographers collecting oracles (from themselves) on how to behave, the Abrahamic fantasy has come down to this: rants, gibberish, and worse. It's hard to say that there's one primary force at the heart of the Islamic brand of monotheism, but one safe suggestion is what Kant called the dear self. The Qur'an is saturated with Muhammad's hypersensitive ego: Forgetting that a good wine needs no bush, he keeps praising his own handiwork as "glorious,"(85:21—and four other times) "perfected"(11:1), and "flawless" (39.28): "Those who fear their Lord tremble with awe at its revelations, and their skins and hearts melt at the remembrance of God" (39.23). Muhammad is forever challenging unnamed critics to produce anything nearly as good as his work (92:23), which, he declares in the very first verse after the Exordium "must not be doubted" (2:1). Elsewhere it's described as "easy to remember" (54:32), "a book of guidance for mankind" (2:284), and coming straight from God (4:82). Best of all, "He that obeys the Apostle obeys God" (4:80), hence, "The only true faith in God's sight is Islam" (3:19). (As surely as no one has ever washed and waxed a rental car, no religion in the history of the world has ever advertised itself as second- or third-best.)

Accordingly, those accept the Qur'an must be very privileged indeed. And, by golly, they *are*: "You are the noblest community ever raised up for mankind" (3:110), bound for the exquisite delights of Paradise (which do not, alas, include winter sports, since Muhammad had never skied, skated, or sledded). So, as we've seen, the reflected glory from the Holy One, the only true God, unlike the blasphemous Christian Trinity (5:73), and his Prophet, spills all over believers, so long as they submit, submit, submit. As with Christianity, no intellectual discernment, or practically none, is required. Just believe as Abraham did—Abraham, by the way, gets far more attention in the Qur'an than in the New Testament; and Muhammad named his only son Ibrahim, whom he may have meant to be his successor, as he had been Abraham's; but the boy died at around a year and a half. Abraham, as retailored by Muhammad, turns out to be the model Muslim. It takes a prophet to know a prophet.

And there is no bigger Abrahamic ceremony anywhere in the world than in the Eid Al-Adha, celebrating the "noble sacrifice" (37:106) that substituted a sheep for Ishmael. Readers wishing to see the slaughter in all its glory would have to go to Mecca. Non-Muslims and others unable to make the hajj can google "Eid Al-Adha sacrifices" and get at least a glimpse of the blood-soaked orgies. There is also the sensitive commentary of Abdellah Hammouni, a Moroccan-born Princeton psychologist who made the hajj in 1999, and who writes in *A Season in Mecca: Narrative of a Pilgrimage* (2006):

> I knew the gaze of these penned-in beasts too well. I could remember the flight, the panic, the questing eye of animals seized for the slaughter at the abattoirs I had seen in my youth. I could hear the heartrending bleats, the pleas rising to the sky with the steam and swell of hot blood. These same scenes would be repeated the next day, the day of sacrifice; millions of creatures were waiting to be put to death.
> In Mina, the sheds looked like a giant concentration camp for animals: two, three, four million heads or more. An immense crowd of pilgrims was preparing to sacrifice them as an "offertory," along with the sacrifices of expiation or alms.

> No matter how many times I reminded myself of what differentiates us from animals domestic and wild, no matter how I widened this distance by thinking about faceless, speechless spe-

cies, incapable—as we imagine it—of expressing emotion, still the mingled scent of blood, excrement and sweat once again gripped me by the throat. We were gathered here to save our own lives, a salvation requiring that we kill these animals. The mass of pilgrims, who had reached the peak of renunciation—after the station of Arafat, the prayer at Muzdalifah, and the stoning at Mina—was about to snuff out millions of lives. Maybe it's true that when I first saw an animal I saw a generic type. Yet each act of immolation put an end to a life as singular as any human life; it was an act of violence—murder, in a word. (pp. 222-223)

Hammoudi's companion, Salim, a pious shopkeeper from Taza in Morocco, keeps telling him, "We're going where Ibrahim went, we're walking in his blessed footsteps and imitating our Prophet, who followed the path traced by Ibrahim, the Friend of God. We are imitating them both, may God accept our sacrifice!" Salim couldn't be more religiously accurate; but Hammoudi whose first name means "slave of Allah" can't get in the right devotional mood and irritates Salim by refusing a chunk of the splendid ram he has just had butchered (to cries of—what else?—"God is great!") Vegetarian or just animal-friendly monotheists have always had a hard time: they are, after all, looking God's gift sheep in the mouth and explicitly claiming like Yonah Meir, in I.B. Singer's "The Slaughterer," to be more compassionate than God himself—which actually isn't that difficult.

But Muhammad was a hearty carnivore and bade his followers be the same. And Muhammad strongly identified with Abraham, who had been surrounded by polytheists, and he even made a gesture to win them over with his notorious Satanic verses—only to withdraw those few kind words for the goddesses, Al-Lāt, Al-'Uzzā, and Manāt, and return to his usual mode of mockery (53:22) and detestation (29:25) when speaking of idolaters. There was no need to introduce the covenantal sign of circumcision, because the Arabs already practiced it, and no need to justify the wholly masculine shape of Islam. Female genital mutilation predated Islam too; but it has become deeply entrenched in African Muslim countries, and is now making advances in Indonesia.

In "A Cutting Tradition," *New York Times,* January 28, 2008, Sarah Corbett describes the work of the Assalaam Foundation, which provides free clitoridectomies to Indonesian girls in Bandung, operations that run the gamut from pinpricks to butchery. On the day Corbett visited, some 200 girls were "treated," many appearing to be younger than five. The chairman of the foundation, Lukman Hakim, held forth on the reasons why clitoridectomy is good for girls: "One, it will stabilize her libido; two, it will make a woman look more beautiful in the eyes of her husband. And three, it will balance her psychology." Some Muslim apologists have lately been responding to western outrage over FGM by insisting that it has no place in Qur'an. True, but why has Islamic cultural space been so receptive to FGM over the centuries? Monotheism has always and indisputably been a guy-thing; but Muslims added a new dimension of female subjugation.

And then there was the problem of prophets. The Jews venerated Moses, but over time they became leery of prophets because of their radical individualism and their habit of claiming that God had personally approved everything they said and did. In the end, normative Judaism dropped the whole thing, and at some point in the third century BCE we find the stunning oracle in Zechariah 13.2, where Yahweh equates prophets and "unclean spirits," and swears to drive both "out of the land." But the Christians showed that you could build an entire religion around a super-prophet, especially when his message was a welcome one. After all, most people were happy to worship the Power that protected the tribe (broadly understood) and promised bodacious rewards in the sweet by-and-by. The ultimate proof of the deity's favoritism was the spread of the worshiping community, by fertility, conquest, or conversion. And Islam did sensationally well in all those departments.

At the heart of the process was a magic book. It may have been that to the illiterate Muhammad and his mostly analphabetic cohort, there was something nearly miraculous about writing and books, long before the incalculable proliferation of the printed word had made talk, in more than one sense, cheap. In any case, all the Abrahamic religions fostered their own cult of the Inspired Prophet and the Sacred Word, now so deeply engrained in Muslims that a cartoon of the Prophet or word of the Qur'an's being profaned is enough to unleash a murderous mob against persons at best remotely connected with the profaner. The bottom line to all this, as ever, is absurdity; but by general agreement we must honor, respect, and refrain from criticizing the believers who engage in such vile behavior. To which one can only respond: Why?

With the Islamic version of Abrahamism, the third time's the charm: the ancient paradigm can now be seen in all its morbidity as a narcissistic *Männersache*. Although God's "decisions" are not supposed to be questioned, the inventions and borrowings of the Prophet demand to be scrutinized, especially since they reproduce so many dubious patterns from the bad old days of monotheism. What sense does it make for The Divine Master of the Universe to have chosen an individual (and his tribe) for preferential treatment? The self-serving, chauvinistic nature of this delirious dream can't be missed.

Muhammad, for example, repeatedly marvels at the fact that the Qur'an is in Arabic (as if Allah had any other options whilst conversing with his monolingual prophet), and "eloquent" (16:103, 26:196), "free from any flaw" (39:28) at that. So magical is the text that to this day some non-Arab Muslim children are taught to memorize and recite it without knowing the meaning of the words (like more than a few bar mitzvah candidates and pre-Vatican II altar boys). Once that flawless revelation has been delivered, the process of proselytizing begins: propaganda, missionary work, and—where needed—forced conversion. (See the age-old Ottoman practice of *devşirme*, the kidnapping and Islamization of Christian children, just like the custom of baptizing pagans en masse by European missionaries.)

The end result, ideally and often in fact, is mass worship: a million and more people gathered in front of Mecca's Masjid al-Haram, the throngs of men jammed together in mosques, flinging themselves periodically to the floor in the world's most famous gesture of submission. The individual merges with the tribe, and the tribe abases itself before the Almighty Lord, thereby paradoxically magnifying itself beyond measure and acquiring invincible strength for the struggle against its enemies. For both Christianity and Islam, the very existence of unbelievers is at best a painful reminder of an uncompleted task, and at worst a continuous scandal. (Jews have long since resigned themselves to being a tiny community, with rules that are too arcane and bothersome to ever have wide appeal.)

Efforts to convert the unbelievers might be interpreted as a generous wish to spread the perceived blessings enjoyed by the faithful (though only God can give faith). And there's something to that. But there's no escaping the group-egoism in such "outreach" (and the dudgeon arising from its rejection). Note, for example, the classic Muslim response to word of the latest terrorist atrocity: again and again "spokesmen" or just passers-by will say, "That's not Islamic," meaning "No *real* Muslim does/did/would do something like this." Which, in turn, breaks down into either a) the perpetrator(s) betrayed the true spirit of Islam, or b) no Muslim actually did this, because a Muslim by definition *couldn't ever* be guilty of such behavior, because everything Islamic is by definition virtuous and good, even as the Qur'an is the undiluted essence of truth (hence the enormously popular Islamic urban legend that the 9/11 attacks must have been carried out the Mossad).

By this adamantine circular reasoning, what Muslims do *as* Muslims is right because they're doing what Allah, speaking through Muhammad, told them to do; and *that* is always right because Allah is always right, because he's Allah. Allah's commands are undoubtedly perfect because his prophet Muhammad said so; and Muhammad said so because Allah told him so. Any questions? Abraham plays a crucial role here as the primordial instance of how all this craziness works: God booms his orders and promises out of nowhere (i.e., the hypersensitive subconscious of a troubled, restive male). We hear Abraham's story and identify with it.

But you couldn't take this God seriously if he didn't have a terrifying side (we've already noted the impossibility of a feminine Almighty God). So Allah and Yahweh "before" him incinerate the gay goons of Sodom and Gomorrah, and have the right to demand the lifeblood of Isaac, among other first-born sons. You *have* to approach this God (or respond when he approaches you) with fear and trembling. On the other hand, God needs Abraham as much as Abraham needs him: How is an invisible deity going to get any respect from humans unless Abraham and his offspring establish and promote his cult? So we have a classic kind of co-dependency.

Once the Mysterious Voice has taken on a personality of its own, e.g., supplied with a basso profondo voice, a keen poetic eye, and a batch of rhetorical tropes (but zero sense of humor), the Grand Transaction between humanity and the imagined deity can begin. It's a feedback loop that has led to, among other things, the belief and practices of some 1.6 billion Muslims, nearly a quarter of the human race. Needless to say,, that still puts them behind the world's 2.2 billion Christians; but, from a secular point of view, the Muslim presence is harder to ignore and put up with.

The problem is that, unlike a high percentage of both Christians and Jews, too many Muslims still take their Abrahamic delusions seriously. Stuck in its medieval time-warp, Islam has yet to undergo the dilution and at least semi-rationalization that Judaism and Christianity (with notable exceptions, of course) have been passing through ever since the Enlightenment. *Le siècle des lumières* has unfortunately been taking its time to arrive in the lands that saw the birth and spread of Qur'anic wisdom. The famous 2002 United Nations report on Human Development in the Arab world noted that all the Arab countries together, with some 270 million people, were translating some 330 foreign language books a year, whilst underdeveloped Greece, with a population of 11 million, was translating five times as many.

Given such monumental ignorance, it's no wonder that untold millions of Muslims would read the Qur'an literally and uncritically, or that they would react with such predictable fury to any perceived insult to the Prophet, the Qur'an, and Islam (i.e., themselves). A Muslim mob will occasionally assault Christians (e.g., in Egypt, Sudan, Iraq, or Pakistan). Countless Muslims continue to manifest their Allah-based approval for antiquated sexual repression, crude and violent homophobia, virulent Jew-hatred, and the veiling, imprisoning, and disempowerment of women. No visible female hair! No dating! No mixed bathing! No mixed working! No mixed learning! No skimpy athletic shorts and tops! No form-fitting clothes! No living or traveling alone! No consulting with male doctors! And, in the Prophet's ultra-pious homeland, no driving!

Amid such backwardness (though it be the height of political incorrectness to call it that), finding a credible Muslim liberal is difficult. For instance, trilingual (Arabic, French, English) author and professor Tarik Ramadan is often cited as the near-ideal intermediary between Islam and the West; but examination of his public dicta (e.g., his call for a "moratorium" on stoning for adultery) isn't encouraging. Speaking at an American Academy of Religion meeting in Montreal (see Allan Nadler, "Tariq Ramadan Gets Hero's Welcome, and Cold Shoulder, at Religion Scholar Conferences," *The Jewish Daily Forward* (11/22/2009), Ramadan said that, "The best way to transform the position of women in Islam is to go back and look to the life of the Prophet and how he treated his wives." Sure thing.

Elsewhere, the highly respected (and far less controversial) Prof. Seyyed Hossein Nasr (Islamic Studies, George Washington University," writes in his amiably entitled *The Heart of Islam: Enduring Values for Humanity* (2002) that, "The rights of God" stand above the rights of human beings, and for a person to insult the religion of others is not considered a right at all, even if the prevention of such an act decreases one's individual rights." (*Tant pis* for Salman Rushdie.) "The same holds true for questions of morality, including sexual morality ..." Nasr cites Titus Burckhardt's support for Islam's acceptance of polygyny and rejection of polyandry, along with the right of Muslim men, but not women, to marry Christians or Jews: "Man, as spiritual officiant (*imām*) of his family, represents the Truth; his role corresponds to the 'active' vessel, namely the Spirit, whereas his wife corresponds to the 'passive' vessel, namely the soul." Muslim philosophers and theologians, it seems, aren't ready to settle down in the Secular City.

But you can't blame them for that. There's at least one very good reason for resisting modernity: As the history of the separation of church and state in Europe has shown, once religion becomes just another merchant trying to make a sale in the marketplace of ideas, a high-tone club-cum-lobby, it's almost guaranteed to lose power, influence, and numbers. Just check to see how many non-tourists can be found in the great cathedrals and basilicas of France, Italy, etc. on any given day. Even in America, where Mormons, evangelicals, and others (e.g., Texas governor Rick Perry calling for three days of prayer in 2011 to halt the fires sweeping his drought-stricken state) want to tear down the not-so-imposing wall between Church and state, the churches have had to forgo their once dominant role. It's been a relatively short time since large populations anywhere were free to bail out of the religious community they were born into; and once acquired, that freedom won't be readily relinquished.

On the other hand, there's no denying the power of denial. For millennia now Jews and Christians have ignored, excused, or lied about all the errors, contradictions, and absurdities in *their* Holy Books and timeless creeds. They've professed nonsense about imaginary angels, incredible miracles, non-existent Messiahs, worlds-to-come that won't ever come, inconceivable Immaculate Conceptions, and so forth. They've picked and chosen the happiest highlights (the return from Exile in Babylon) while passing over in the silence the unmentionable or embarrassing parts (Joshua's genocides). They've confused the ideal community (Christianity, the heavenly Jerusalem) with the actual one (Christendom, Southern Baptists, etc.)

But over the past few centuries liberal and less-than-Orthodox Jewish and Christians have been positively influenced by secular currents promoting such things as democracy, tolerance, freedom of speech, gender equality, and respect for science, which were never part of their original "divine" charter. Muslims, by contrast, have been relatively more hostile than their elder monotheistic brethren. For example, the vast majority of Muslims strongly reject Darwinism (see Salman Hameed, "Bracing for Islamic Creationism," *Science*, Dec. 12, 2008—not that they understand it any more than creationists).

In their benighted faith-state Muslims remind us of the larger truth, long disguised by Jews and Christians, that Abrahamism and honest empiricism are incompatible. You can't believe that truth emerges both from hard, fiercely contested work in the laboratory of experience *and* from unfathomable, mysterious Voices delivering flawless, immortal oracles to self-proclaimed prophets. There must be a better way: there is, and it's called rationality, aka the opposite of miracle, mystery, and authority, so forcefully put down by that obnoxious reactionary Dostoyevsky in "The Grand Inquisitor" (even though he adored those forces as much as anyone).

It's the monotheistic "trinity" miracle = what can't happen; mystery = what can't be explained or even talked sensibly about; authority = the power to enforce an awed response to the above mumbo-jumbo. All this is on display in Abrahamism, and with special splendor in contemporary Islam, with its sky-high levels of credulity. Why shouldn't we believe, as most Muslims do, that the Ka'aba was originally built by Adam, restored by Noah, and fixed up again by Abraham and Ishmael? Why *wouldn't* the most earth-shaking events of all time take place in the tribe's backyard? (Try to visualize the Ka'aba perched on the Jersey shore.) Why *wouldn't* a few murky bits of folklore about a supposed Grand Ancestor be the key to the meaning of life? Why *wouldn't* the master of the Universe be drawn to make a treaty with *our* non-Jewish, non-Christian (2:140) Sheikh/Patriarch and his # 1 son? Why *wouldn't* it be the sacred duty of all other tribes and peoples on earth to buy into our divinely patented version of The Truth, as shown by our own Prophet Muhammad's irrefragable testimony, expressed in the finest classical Arabic? It's as clear as a sunny day in Mecca.

Conclusion

Farewell to the Lunacy

And he [Saul] went thither to Naioth in Ramah; and the Spirit of God was upon him also, and he went on, and prophesied ... And he stripped off his clothes also, and prophesied before Samuel in like manner, and lay down naked all that day and all that night. Wherefore they say, "Is Saul also among the prophets?"

—1 Sam. 19.23-24

An auditory hallucination or *paracusia* is a form of hallucination that involves perceiving sounds without auditory stimulus. A common form involves hearing one or more talking voices. This may be associated with psychiatric disorders such as schizophrenia or mania, and holds special significance in diagnosing these conditions. However, individuals may hear voices without suffering from diagnosable mental illness. The Hearing Voices Movement is a support and advocacy group for people who do hallucinate but otherwise show no signs of mental illness or impairment.

—Wikipedia, "Auditory Hallucination"

As we prepare to say goodbye to Abraham and his followers, it might be useful to imagine the following scene: a squad car is cruising through a large public park, and at a turn in the road the cops spot an old man with a large knife bending over the supine body of a kid, who has been tightly bound and laid out on a rock. Upon approaching, stopping, and questioning the (really) old man, he tells them that he heard a voice telling him to sacrifice the lad (who, despite the scores of years separating them, turns out to be his son) to an invisible "God," who has been "appearing" and "speaking" to him for some years now. How many seconds before they disarm the old man? How many minutes before he's handcuffed and taken to the station? How many hours before he's been diagnosed as a schizophrenic and put under 24-hour surveillance? Oh wait—he's not a psychopath, he's a transcendent genius and the founder of monotheism. Sorry about that.

If we remove the thick coating of age-old veneration, it's pretty easy to see that the far-famed spokesmen of the great Guy God (who rarely says a word to or about women, except to issue rules on how to control them) and the most popular Middle-Eastern deity, that these prophets, whether real or imaginary figures, were, for lack of a more precise term, crazy. But back in the old days individuals who were "touched" in this way often stirred up feelings of fear and wonder in their fellows; and it seems easy to reconstruct the progress of their delusions. As the subjects of such astonishing "visitations," the prophets (Abraham, Moses, Jesus, Paul, Muhammad, et al.) would inevitably have enjoyed both a surge in self-importance and a wave of veneration from their superstitious listeners.

Consider one of the best-known examples of such supposed communications with the divine, part of Paul's "boast" in 2 Corinthians: "I will come to visions and revelations of the Lord. I knew a man in Christ above fourteen years ago, whether in the body I cannot tell, or whether out of the body, I cannot tell, God knoweth:

such a one, caught up to the third heaven. And I knew such a man (whether in the body or out of the body, I cannot tell, God knoweth), how that he was caught up into paradise, and heard unspeakable words, which it is not lawful for a man to utter" (12.2-4) Paul is only bringing these things up to quiet his opponents in Corinth and reassert his God-given authority; but he admits that he got more than a little high on the whole thing, and then, "Lest I should be exalted above measure through the abundance of the revelation, there was given to me a thorn in the flesh, the messenger of Satan to buffet me, lest I should be exalted above measure" (v. 7). Nobody knows that who or what "the thorn" or "the messenger of Satan" was; but the general idea, that he had a transcendentally privileged experience, is plain enough. He went on a trip that we ordinary, caught-in-the-rush-hour mortals can only dream of.

Neither Abraham, Moses (*pace* the Bible-screamers), nor Jesus ever wrote any memoirs; so we have less direct evidence about them. But Paul and Muhammad talked a lot about themselves, Muhammad obsessively so, which leaves us with a lot of evidence. Among the recurrent notes in the sacred texts about the Founders is that of divinely assigned and unique greatness. Yahweh has barely begun to address Abraham for the first time when he tells him that, "I will make of thee a great nation, and I will bless thee, and make thy name great; and thou shalt be a blessing" (Gen. 12.2). Naturally it was only a matter of time before the synagogue morning service would include thanks to God for not having made the (male) congregant a gentile (*shelo asani goy*), a slave, or a woman. Christians have always repeated the formula from Acts 4.12, "Neither is there salvation in any other [than Jesus], for there is no other name under heaven given among men, whereby we must be saved." And Muhammad is even more insistent that, "The only true faith in God's eyes is Islam" (3:19), and "He that chooses a religion other than Islam, it will not be accepted from him and in the world to come he will surely be among the losers" (3:85). (One can just see the hosts of disgruntled infidels tearing up and discarding their worthless tickets in the Heavenly Hippodrome.)

So it's established: Our God is the greatest. One of the reasons why the relatively easy-going henotheism of early sacred history has to be tossed out is to broaden the distance separating the worshipers of The One True God from those who adore one or more from the cheesy-rotten competition. If *we* have the only God there is, *they* have nothing. As we've seen at every step of the way, the ego-component of monotheism is enormous. It's the ultimate mutual admiration society.

All the emphasis on sin and God's anger at it might seem to be a dark, depressing shadow over this picture; but God takes a special interest in sinners, as long as they come around eventually. As Ezekiel says (18.21-23), "But if the wicked will turn from all his sins that he hath committed and keep all my statutes, and do that which us lawful and right, he shall not die. All his transgressions that he hath committed, they shall not be mentioned unto him: in his righteousness that he hath done he shall live. Have I any pleasure at all that the wicked should die?" Paul and Muhammad agree: "Where sin abounded, grace did much more abound" (Rom. 5.20). "If you repent, it shall be well with you" (9:3). Sinners are more colorful than saints, even as the "twice-born" have better stories to tell than the "once-born" (see James's *Varieties of Religious Experience*). The riches of God's mercy are infinite—just make sure to beg for them in a timely fashion.

Similarly, sacrifice, whether animal or human, physical or "spiritual," plays a more positive role in the Abrahamic God-man encounter than one might think—even though God is the supreme example of the person who has everything and hence no need or use for things like blood, smoke, or burning fat. Naturally, any "gift" to God—and the more precious, the better—endears man to God. Religious, and especially ascetical, life often seems to be a contest to see who can go to the most heroic lengths in despoiling himself (or, in Christianity, making himself suffer) for the Almighty. But the converse is also true: making hard, even unendurable sacrifices to God endears him to *us*. The devotee has gone above and beyond the call of duty, and feels all the better of himself for it. Even if Abraham gets Isaac back unharmed (or resurrected after being burned to ashes), he was morally willing to lose him forever; and it's the intention that matters. In Christianity, Jesus is the sacrificial victim; but all believers are called on to be victims like him, to take up their cross and follow the Master (Mt. 16.24). thus becoming at once sacrificing fathers and sacrificial sons. For Muslims animal sacrifices would be sufficient; but the hajj itself is a repetition of Abraham's journey to sacrifice Ishmael, down to such details as casting stones at Satan in memory of Abraham's conquering the diabolical temptation *not* to offer up his son. Thus, pilgrims, and perhaps Muslims as a group, identify still more with Abraham than either Jews or Christians do.

Now that the covenant has been fully ratified, God and man are in business as never before. Through a process of loving imitation, the mass of ordinary believers can try to recreate in themselves the Prophet's experience as related in the Holy Book or else settle for tender veneration of the Man and his God. Naturally, they can't have the same experiences he had because then there'd be a proliferation of prophets, and who knows what new divine messages might emerge—the chaos that gave rise to all sort of heresies and craziness, like the Anabaptists, the Shakers, the Mormons, etc.

But banning newcomers from the magic circle of prophethood does nothing to lessen the egocentricity of Abrahamic religion. What God demands above all is exclusive worship—which why he keeps calling himself "jealous," and his followers keep returning the favor by abusing and persecuting the acolytes of all alternative deities. Why he should want that is hard to say. Given his infinite intellect, how could he be interested in our confused, childish mutterings (whose every syllable he can predict in advance anyway)?

Does he grin and bear our banal, repetitive acts of self-obeisance because he knows it's good for us? Mustn't it all get *really* boring? In any case, why should we spend time flattering (or glorifying or beseeching) him? Animals don't engage in anything remotely resembling worship; and their lives don't seem any the worse for it.

But perhaps worship is just another form of love (God *is* love, says 1 John 4.16, though the obverse apparently isn't true). Augustine famously puzzled about what he loved when he loved God, coming up with statements that Huck Finn would have found in his role as occasional theologian "interesting but tough": "Not the beauty of any corporal thing; not the order of times, nor the brightness of the light which we do behold, so gladsome to our eyes: not the pleasant melodies of songs of all kinds; nor the fragrant smell of flowers, and ointment, and spices: not manna and honey; nor any fair limbs that are so acceptable to fleshly embracements. I love none of these things whenas I love my God: and yet I love a certain kind of light, and a kind of voice, and a kind of fragrance, and a kind of meat [food], and a kind of embracement, wheneas I love my God" (*Confessions* X, vi, tr. William Watts).

Defining "a kind of" proves impossible; but at least Augustine makes it clear that there's some sort of payoff. (Pure apophatic theology is intellectually cool, but emotionally it's a washout.) And that might recall a basic point to be found in Nietzsche's *Human, All Too Human*, (1878) where he quotes the German physicist and wit George Lichtenberg (d. 1799): "It's impossible, as the saying goes, for us to *feel* for others; we feel only for ourselves. That statement sounds harsh, but it isn't, if you understand it the right way. We don't love either father or mother or wife or child, we love the pleasant feelings they provoke in us" (133). And then Nietzsche echoes Georg Lichtenberg with a line from La Rochefoucauld: "*Si on croit aimer sa maîtresse pour l'amour d'elle, on est bien trompé,*" that is, we love people for what we get from them. One of the reasons for monotheism's popularity is the way it allows individuals to think they've escaped the limits of selfhood, even as generous donors on telethons are allowed to revel in their selfless charity.

Fantasizing that we're in contact with something resembling the LORD Abraham supposedly "met" induces pleasurable sensations (even awe and terror have their pleasures). The "God" may be, in fact is, fictional; but the feelings are real. And they convey a primordial sense of security and importance. Of course, the messages and faiths of Abraham, Jesus-Paul, and Muhammad are incompatible with one another, as the great majority of their followers have always thought and said. Jews need no prophets beyond their own. Christians need no prophet except Jesus (and his explicators), even as they like to think of all previous Hebrew prophets as pointing to HIM. Muslims likewise see all prophets as leading up to *theirs*, without whom the predecessors are incomplete. Abraham, if he existed, would undoubtedly be surprised to see the ways that Christians and Muslims have made him over, though presumably he would also have been amazed by the vast new body of law making up Moses' covenant.

In any event, the three "faiths" don't fit together, as the briefest look at current hard-line versions of them all will show: *Haredim*, conservative Evangelicals, and Salafists. These are, it goes without saying, the kind of extremists that their embarrassed liberal co-religionists, speaking irenically in the public arena, will decry as unrepresentative of the best their traditions have to offer. That's the whole point of endless ecumenical celebration of all things Abrahamic. But enlightened theological commentators—to cite three recent distinguished examples, people like Rabbi Daniel E. Polish, Prof. Patrick Ryan, S.J., and Prof. Amir Husain, who have engaged in a series of public ecumenical conversations sponsored by Fordham University—don't seem to realize that once you begin compromising with the primitive core of your sacred texts, sooner or later the whole superstructure is going to collapse.

Of course, the primary thrust of modernity is toward rational thinking, relativizing, and rejecting claims of absolute certainty. But applying these principles to monotheism is like letting blasts of fresh air into the mummy's tomb: the fragile relics start to crumble. You mean, Sarah *wasn't* ninety years old when she got pregnant, as Scripture says (Gen. 17.17)? You mean Jesus *wasn't* born of a virgin? You mean, God, "the Compassionate, the Merciful" was literally full of hot air when he told his trembling prophet that, "Garments of fire have been prepared for the unbelievers. Scalding water shall be poured upon their heads, melting their skin and that which is in their bellies. They shall be lashed with rods of iron" (22:19)? Uh-oh.

The issues here couldn't be simpler: either there are magical texts, or there aren't. Since no perfect text has ever been found, and since the Jewish, Christian, and Muslim scriptures are full, not just of errors but of howlers and *longueurs*, they don't qualify as perfect or anything resembling it. Nor does it make sense to talk about an almost-magical text or a nearly-perfect text with some unfortunate crummy parts. Who's in charge here anyway, the reader or the text? So long as the reader reserves the right to pass judgment on the text, he or she is asserting control over it. And that means knowing—as millions of readers do—that countless secular writers have composed texts far more engrossing than the liturgical prescriptions of Exodus and Leviticus; that countless moralists have made wiser remarks than Ephesians 6.5, "slaves, obey your earthly masters with fear and trembling" (NRSV); and that at least a large minority, if not an actual majority, of all the books ever written are better organized than the Qur'an.

Once the fortress door is opened to non-worshipful criticism, it's basically game over. Mysterious stories that have to be revered just because previous generations always revered them now need to face serious scrutiny. A book that tells us there was once a man named Abraham about whom it was said that he said that he once heard a voice from somebody called God saying the most amazing things, and further says that this God is the master, not merely of the Abraham and his family, but of a tribe, of many tribes, of all history, and of the entire universe—such a book has got to arouse intense suspicion, along with skeptical contempt. Oh really?

The story's structural elements, as we've seen, break down quickly into elements of schizophrenic fantasy, personal and group self-aggrandizement, sectarian borrowing (by Paul and Muhammad, among others), Oedipal problems overcome, and institutionalized happy-ever-aftering. One gigantic fiction, one gigantic folly. The obvious healthy alternative to all this is that when someone—an actual person, not an imagined one—claims to have heard voices from the beyond, don't argue. Just call a doctor.

Meanwhile, what to do about the multifarious religious institutions and their spokesmen (not women—quick, name the world's three most eminent female religious leaders, name just one) still occupying large chunks of public space (in the USA at least)? Actually, there are two ways of looking at this. On the one hand, the country is still, at this late date, saturated with monotheism, even as the landscape is dotted (pimpled?) with synagogues, churches, and mosques. On April 10, 2011, for example, the New York Times paperback Bestseller List had three religious titles in the top ten: *Heaven is For Real* by Todd Burpo with Lynn Vincent (a child's vision of the Beyond), *Have a Little Faith* by the endlessly inspirational Mitch Albom, and *90 Minutes in Heaven* by Don Pipe with Cecil Murphey (a minister's blissed-out near-death experience).

God is celebrated on courtroom walls and our currency, in the Pledge of allegiance and the witness's oath. You can't aspire to any national office without some kind of ecclesio-theological affiliation, however flimsy. Politicians have to address all tragic situations, from a death in the family to a terrorist attack, with their "thoughts and prayers." The media always speak of religion with hushed reverence—any kind of fanatical biblical faith, short of Westboro Baptist Church's transparently self-seeking shenanigans, will get a free pass. Multicultural academics who prefer diversity to hopelessly tainted terms like "intelligence" or "talent," are forever praising religion, even if they themselves would never be caught dead inside a house of worship. While resisting incursions by Bible-belters into secular public realms, they are ultra-polite about religion, especially the non-western kind, since that's part of culture; and one never criticizes another person's culture.

So, Americans are agreed: "faith-based" is good, like "God-given," and the always handy "good Lord." On a less dogmatic level they give more or less unanimous approval to religiously tinged "values," "beliefs," "traditions," and, best of all, spirituality (impossible to define, but always precious). And in the realm of pseudo-philosophy there's the inevitable, "You know, I believe"—meaningful pause—"everything happens for a reason," which in its literal sense might sound unimpeachable, but which is actually a tongue-tied, dumbed-down paraphrase of Tennyson's desperate cry, "O, yet we trust that somehow good/ Will be the final goal of ill,/ ... That nothing walks with aimless feet, That not one life shall be destroyed,/ Or cast as rubbish to the void/When God hath made the pile complete." That monumental pile (the New Jerusalem. the Kingdom of God on earth, whatever) is much farther from completion than it was nearly two centuries ago, when Tennyson began mourning his beloved Hallam; but the trope of "trust" is still *de rigueur* in American public discourse.

On the other hand, it could be argued that in the USA most of Matthew Arnold's "sea of faith" (like Kazakhstan's Aral Sea) has either dried up or is pathetically shallow. The younger generation is increasingly turned off by institutional religion and its timeworn biases (misogyny, homophobia, etc.) The nation's largest denomination, the Catholic Church, is in near-total disarray. Comedians like Bill Maher, Stephen Colbert, or the South Park gang feel free to mock Jehovah & Co. Neo-atheism is flourishing with writers like Sam Harris or the late Christopher Hitchens and, more to the point, Richard Dawkins and Daniel Dennett, saying things that multitudes of scientists and educated people have said for ages, but only sotto voce, because the time wasn't ripe. And, speaking of time, has there been a major religious artist of any kind for the last fifty years? In view of all that, why not just sit back and relax while the remaining pools of religion evaporate?

Well, for one thing, that scenario is far too rosy. For another, intellectual honesty demands continued resistance to the monotheists despite the many fine individuals who persist, out of old habit, uncritical carelessness, or garden-variety nostalgia, in clinging to the Abrahamite tradition, whose decaying components can be dealt with under the headings of this-worldly and otherworldly. "This-worldly" comprises all the public and private doings of religious institutions, some of which, of course, are valuable, like hospitals, or at least partly beneficial, like schools that teach the three Rs along with the foolish fourth, religion. But Abrahamism is basically such a tissue of errors and absurdities that its net effect has to be rated as negative. Humanitarianism can get along perfectly well without it; and rational morality does much better without it, as seen from the long centuries of support (or silent acquiescence) that devout Abrahamites have given to political oppression, war, male ownership of women, environmental devastation, vindictive penal systems, and the countless shapes and guises of animal cruelty.

"Otherworldly" covers the range of fantasies about a mysterious extra dimension (the holy, the sacred, the divine, the transcendent, the spiritual, and similar breathless labels) that supposedly undergirds or overarches or compenetrates the everyday empirical world. This above-and-beyond domain, associated perforce with the sky and outer space, is utterly superior to everything in our sublunary digs, which it invades from time to time to greet, threaten, reward or punish us. Or so we're told. Even though such events are exceedingly rare (i.e., never occur at all), they serve to remind us that the banal transactions of daily existence in which we're so absorbed shrink to utter insignificance when compared with godly operations, even as our greatly overrated planet is in truth a minor appendage to the much vaster heavenly realm or, as the Jews call it, *olam ha-emet.*

The stories of Abraham are all about the imaginary invasion of the here-and-now by the (non-existent) "Eternal," an idea as unhealthy as it is unfounded. The roots of this illusion probably lie in the childish—and grown-up—habit of assigning human or humanlike agents to all phenomena, as in the ancient Greek phrase "Zeus is raining" to mean "It's raining." In a similar vein, Latin poets would write "Mars," "Venus," "Neptune," and "Minerva," to mean "war," "sex," "the sea," and "wisdom," without literally believing in such anthropomorphic deities. In the child's world things happen mostly because adults make them happen; so it stands to reason that some mighty personal power must lie behind all natural events, and a fortiori behind any events thought to be extraordinary, like the survival of the Jews, the resiliency of Christianity, or the spread of Islam.

And there would be no surprise if this "Force" (as in *Star Wars*) were to speak, conveniently enough in our own dialect, to us or to some particularly gifted individuals. They would have to have extra-sensitive nervous systems, like the real or fictional Abraham, or Paul, or Muhammad, to pick up the divine signals that to most others were very faint or totally imperceptible. Encouraged by their example, myriads of their followers, hitherto marginally attuned, if at all, to "the Lord," would be eager to imitate the prophets and get in on the celestial conversation. The rest is religious history.

At this point someone has to blow a loud whistle, which is precisely what European thinkers—Hume, Marx, Feuerbach, Nietzsche, Durkheim, Freud, etc—have been doing since the Enlightenment. (And, by the way, it's impossible to miss the disproportionate numbers of God's first chosen people who philosophically bit the hand that fed them.) But the rationalists can berate the believers all they want: there was no stifling the literal en-thus-iasm of people who felt or liked to think that they had been visited from on high. This belief is self-reinforcing, as when a group of students informed that they are "advanced" (regardless of their actual test scores), promptly begin to perform better. Having been told that they were unique (a move that in itself took some daring), the Jews likewise began to feel and act unique—and continue to do so thousands of years later, though now often with no reference to "the Name" that once made it all possible.

But once the "divine" impetus of sacred history falls back into the all-too-human sphere (from which it never actually escaped), it becomes obvious what kind of landscape we're stuck in: the swamp of patriarchalism. The God directing and starring in Abraham's epic story (and its sequels) turns out to be an inflated Daddy-figure (note how Muhammad recoiled in contempt from the very notion of goddesses). Trapped, like everyone else, in their socially shaped imagination, the first Hebrews naturally couldn't conceive of anything bigger or better than a Super-Dad; so that's what they gave us.

As for the primordial Papa himself, given *his* homely origins, he was fated to remain, with minor exceptions, bogged down in a male universe, based on male metaphors, male ways of thinking , and male domination. Thus the Bible's covenants between God and men, its patrilinear genealogies, its long lists of nameless women, from Noah's wife and Jephthah's daughter to Pilate's wife and Peter's mother-in-law, and practically non-existent direct relations to females. And as the Lord, so the prophets: Abraham neither bore, nursed, nor raised Isaac, but he, not Sarah, had the only say about sacrificing the boy. Jesus never bothered to consult with women; and Muhammad ruled his wives as their more or less absolute master (e.g., forbidding them to remarry after his death).

To this day the Abrahamic religions remain the world's largest Men's Club (though they occasionally license some sort of Ladies Auxiliary). Hence the long beards—and the sacred status of male facial hair among conservative monotheists—on Orthodox rabbis, Eastern Orthodox bishops, and mullahs around the world, along with lunatic fringers like the Haredim and Taliban. Meanwhile, in contrast to the righteously hirsute clergy and devout laymen, women in such groups are often made to veil *their* lascivious locks, for fear of distracting the men. St. Paul himself asked the scornful rhetorical question in 1 Cor. 11.13 (RSV), "Is it proper for a woman to pray to God with her head uncovered?" A woman, he declared, *had* to pray veiled, just as a man *had* to pray bareheaded for the obvious reason that, "he is the image and glory [bright reflection] of God; but woman is the glory of man. For man was not made from woman, but woman from man. Neither was man created for woman, but woman for man" (vv.7-8, RSV). Got that? It's a logical consequence of woman's being "a helper fit for him" (Gen. 2.18, RSV), and a future justification for Muhammad's glorious revelation that, "Women are your fields" (2:223).

Hence, apart from a few left-leaning Protestant churches, Abrahamites have systematically excluded women from all positions of power. In the world as we know it, a chief rabbi, pope, or ayatollah with breasts would be unimaginable. (In 2010 the Vatican repeated its ban on ordaining women, calling it a "grave crime.") It figures: A male God must no doubt feel more comfortable with male helpers and associates. And Yahweh- God the Father- Allah is (are) indisputably masculine, just like Elohim, the Pantocrator, the Supreme Judge, the Messiah, Mahdi, etc.

This isn't the fault of all the various pseudo-deities. Everyone committed to, or involved in, Abrahamism has to confront an imaginative impasse here. However defined or pictured, "God" has to be a person, since that's the highest category of life we know; and all the persons (or animals, for that matter) we've ever met are gendered, so God has to be male, female, or—gasp—LBGT. Beyond that, as the most powerful of beings, God has to be thought of as analogous to the people actually holding and exercising power in the human domain. But those people, with a few trivial exceptions like Hillary Clinton or Angela Merkel, are all male and have been since time immemorial. Ergo, God is a man.

And along with women's general inferiority, femalenesss, as both westerners and easterners have always seen it, is burdened with a much heavier sexual freight. The French used to call women *le sexe*. Our term "the fair sex" automatically relegates women to the amatory or coital or decorative realm, whereas maleness is often considered neutral or nearly so. Nowadays, people addressing girls/women in a non-gender-specific way, often say, "you guys." On the other hand, what would nonplussed readers have made of H. Rider Haggard's African adventure novel, if he had entitled it "*He*"? If Mozart had written an opera called *Così fan tutti*, it would have been taken to mean not "Men Are Like That," but "That's What Everyone Does." Guys can transcend their gender, women can't, whence the endless snotty warnings about the perils of PMS in the Oval Office.

When it comes to monotheism, this problem is unfixable, because the foundational texts are engraved in stone, and the prophets who wrote them (or to whom they're attributed) are long dead. Trying to introduce balance and equity into Abrahamite traditions is like trying to fit a racing car spoiler onto a stage coach. Abraham's God is not just grammatically and metaphorically male, "he" inspires the typical response to male power: fear. In Gen. 15.1 God tells Abram to "fear not," evidently because fear would be natural for anyone in his situation. After calling for the Aqedah, Yahweh congratulates Abraham for giving concrete proof of just how much he fears God (22.12). In Gen. 31.42 Jacob will actually call his grandfather's god "the Fear of Isaac." And in Deut. 6.13., right after pronouncing the *Sh'ma*, the very essence of biblical faith,

Moses adds: "Thou shalt fear the LORD thy God, and serve him" How *not* fear a deity who wanted the lives of all firstborn males for himself?

How, after all, could fear *not* be a dominant factor here, given the infinite (imagined) disproportion of power between God and humans? Seeing the face of God—with a few unexplained exceptions—results in death (Ex. 34.20). Hapless Uzzah gets struck dead simply for trying to right the ox cart carrying the Ark of God (2 Sam. 6.7). Aaron's sons Nadab and Abihu are incinerated for the mistake of offering "unholy fire" (Lev. 10.1-2) to the Lord. Korah, Dathan and Abiram, along with 250 of their co-conspirators, accuse Moses of being undemocratic, whereupon they, their wives, children, and grandchildren get swallowed up in the earth or else consumed by fire. Yahweh's angel of death sets a never-to-be-equaled record by slaying 185,000 Assyrians in a single night (1 Kings 19.35), etc. Don't mess with the Lord of Hosts.

Jesus is often thought of as heralding a kinder, gentler God, but that's partly because he's less interested in this world than Yahweh is. His vision of Doomsday has plenty of terror in it. By the time of Jesus, Jews had come to realize that the Lord could no longer be relied on to openly intervene on behalf of his people—except in apocalyptic visions. Scenes like the Exodus or the return from Babylon were gone from the playbook. But as in the imagined mass vendetta for Haman's planned genocide at the end of the Book of Esther, in their climactic Doomsday scenario Christians, like Muslims after them, pictured bloody catastrophes overwhelming their enemies and evil people in general (the two groups tend to fuse). Alas, nowhere in the vast body of eschatological literature are there any reliable percentages of the saved vs. the damned; and the situation is further complicated by the Catholic invention of Purgatory, which seems less sadistic and more practical than hell, but has gotten a chilly reception outside the RCC.

Then too, there's the odd universalist, preaching (eventual) salvation for absolutely all humans; but that seems far too easy-going and relativistic for the omniscient angry Judge we meet in Abrahamic religion. As Revelation 20.11-12 says: "And I saw a great white throne and him that sat on it, from whose face the earth and the heaven fled away, and there was found no place for them. And I saw the dead, small and great, stand before God: and the books were opened; and another book was opened which is the book of life: and the dead were judged out of those things which were written in the books, according to their works." It's hard to imagine the Ancient of Days rolling up the massive print-out of human guilt, tossing it aside, and explaining with a casual shrug, "No problem, folks. We all make mistakes."

What we have, then, in monotheism seems to be an enormous feudal system, with the petty nobility ("inspired" prophets, lawgivers, judges, kings, caliphs, high priests) swearing an oath of loyalty to a glorified projection of themselves, called God or the Lord, which in turn validates their rule over their serfs, the laity or religious amateurs. The Divine Partner agrees (so we are told) to protect and favor his feeble human allies, who promise to sing his praises, sacrifice to, and fight for him. The Covenant can be seen functioning as a military pact in Joshua's fabled campaign against the Canaanites (which wins territory for the Israelites, while YHWH gets to see his rivals put to shame), in the successful parts of the Crusades, Lepanto, and other exploits of Christian imperialism, and in the glorious record of Muslim arms, from the Battle of Badr to 9/11. (True, victories by Christians and Muslims often come at the expense of other monotheistic friends of God, but the losers in each case will just have to sort things out for themselves.)

Beyond the battlefield, the Abrahamic covenants involve, as we have seen, sacred legislation, much of it unjust, wrong-headed or pointless: capital punishment, excessive cruelty, oppression of women, silly ritual requirements, senseless dietary rules, etc. These laws, both those still in force and others long obsolete and unenforced, are grounded on the illusion that God is both the source and criterion of all morality. Abrahamites aren't bothered by the fact that billions of other people have deduced their moral systems from the premise of different deities—or from no deities at all—and that over time major improvements have been made in God's oafish moral code, e.g., abolishing execution for homosexual acts. Believers can ignore such details because, like any other habit, practice of the behaviors inculcated by Abrahamism is self-reinforcing, and quickly becomes self-evident second nature.

As religions grow, they take more elaborate and fantastical twists—see the Haredim way of life or the plight of the deserted orthodox Jewish wife (*agunah*) without divorce papers (*get)*, the culture of Mariolatry or the quaint Catholic doctrine of papal infallibility, the bring-back-the-7th-century Salafist movement or Shiite temporary marriage (*nikah al-tun'ah*), etc. But such bits of random religious madness (all of which also provide down-to-earth payoffs to one group or another) shouldn't distract us from the broader, deeper, grander stretches of lunacy that are the habitat of the Abrahamites.

Not content with the eccentric, narcissistic visions at their core, Judaism, Christianity, and Islam have added libraries of theological speculation, moral casuistry, eschatological dreams, and popular mythology, which add weight and solidity to believers' trajectory, like a ship's ballast or the cement shoes of Mafia victims. It seems safe to predict that in the immediate future the majority of monotheists, especially the older ones, will stick with their irrational doctrines, customs, and rules, despite the silence of the Celestial Oracle, who hasn't said a new word for eons now. Meanwhile, a growing minority, especially the young, will find it much easier to break the Abrahamic covenant and get a life of their own. All it takes, as the Irreverend John Lennon once said, is imagination.

In fact, having opened this tirade with a sort of Lennonesque (in substance if not in style) song, let's close with another:

FADEAWAY

> The master [Baal Shem Tov] used to go to a certain place in the woods and light a fire and pray when he was faced with an especially difficult task—and it was done. His successor, the so-called great Maggid, followed his example and went to the same place, but said: "The fire we can no longer light, the prayer we no longer know; but we can still say the prayer"—and what he asked was done, too. Another generation passed, and Rabbi Moshe Leib of Sassov went into the woods and said: "The fire we can no longer light, and the prayer we no longer know; all we know is the place in the woods, and that will have to be enough." And it was enough. In the fourth generation, Rabbi Israel of Rishin stayed at home and said: "The fire we can no longer light, the prayer we no longer know, nor do we know the place. All we can do is tell the story." According to Agnon, the novelist from whom [Gershom] Scholem got the tale, and according to Buber, too, that proved sufficient.
> They fail to add what the next generation said: "The fire we cannot light, the prayer we do not know, and the place we do not know. We can still tell the story, but we do not believe it."

—Walter Kaufmann, *Critique of Religion and Philosophy* (1958)

Oy, devolution! Going ... gone!
The Shekhinah once brightly shone;
but now it's out, extinguished, poof.
Once everywhere, God's now aloof.
He used to like to shoot the breeze
with us; but it's been centuries
since He last spoke—unless, mayhap,

you count that Book of Mormon* crap.   (*"Chloroform in
   print," Mark Twain said)
And the Qur'an's a boring brew
(no stories†) vis-à-vis the New   (†or very few and all dull)
Testament, itself a feeble sequel
to the Tanakh, no way its equal.

God's maiden speech was thus his best
(but was it *his*? Folks will contest
that point forever, so let's end it:
the Bible's grand, whoever "penned" it—
at least some parts, Job, Psalms, and such,
before the Author lost his touch).
Sure, go ahead, believers, frown:
religion's course is down, down, down.

It starts out with a Golden Age,
when miracles bedeck the stage:
the Red Sea split, sun stood still,
the instant cures without a pill.
Those gorgeous legends (true or not),
those Yahweh-stunts that hit the spot.
But—what a drag—it doesn't last:
The Age of Miracles shoots past
and then can never be repeated
(which leaves believers feeling cheated).
So what to do? Be loud in praise
of wonders from the olden days
(not now, alas, though some have tried,
perhaps faith's batteries have died).

Worse yet, as time goes by, the glow
from God's miraculous flambeau
goes darker: Doubts begin to cluster
"The LORD hath done this!" won't pass muster.
Lit bushes burn, dead men don't rise;
and virgin birth's one weird surprise.
Both Noah's ark and Jonah's whale

are equally beyond the pale.

So shrewd believers, faced with this,
just cry out "Symbol!" and then kiss
the sacred text—Thank God, all's cool!
The obsolete parts? They're a school
of Truth *im Werden* *: Hey, things change:　　(*in development)
goodbye to stoning, *herem* †, angels,　　(†divinely ordered
　　ethnic cleansing)
hell, and all that sexist stuff.
The ancient ways were way too rough.

Hail, demythologized belief!
It brings such wonderful relief
from bunk—and yet, if truth be told,
its temperature runs rather cold.
The fire's doused, the prayer has fled;
no path to find "the place"; instead
beleaguered souls can just retell
the same old stories; but the spell
is broken; mere nostalgia can't
revive the wilted, withered plant
of faith.

　　　　But don't give up the fight,
ye semi-faith-full Sons of Light
(and Daughters too). If you can bear
to swallow such pathetic fare,
such feeble, faded memories
(who else but church mice dig *that* cheese?),
chow down—meanwhile we faith-less cats
(who prowl for reasons, data, stats)
will banquet on much finer food
than Torah and the Holy Rood.
No secret spells, no sacred fire,
no magic stories (and no choir
of bearded *tsaddikim* or saints
to drown out logic's loud complaints):

we'll get some floodlights, maps, and gear
to cross this jungle. Never fear,
we know we won't get out alive,
but whilst exploring we can thrive—
unlike the God-hounds (it's their choice)
still howling for their Master's voice.

—Peter Heinegg

www.ingramcontent.com/pod-product-compliance
Lightning Source LLC
Chambersburg PA
CBHW052133300426
44116CB00010B/1881